Cedar Key
Spirit Tour
A Walk through History

Cedar Key
𝔖𝔭𝔦𝔯𝔦𝔱 𝔗𝔬𝔲𝔯
A Walk through History

by
Debra Lyon-Dye

"Ms Debbie"

Copyright © 2016 by Debra Lyon-Dye, Lazy Dog Publishing
All rights reserved.

LIBRARY OF CONGRESS CATALOG NUMBER 2016912674

Printed in the United States of America

ISBN: 978-1-5323-1551-0

Typography and Book Design by Stephen Wolfsberger
Cover photo used by permission, H. and B. Coulter
All other photos taken by the author

Dedicated to my husband, Danny, who builds up what others have torn down.

Cedar Key Spirit Tour

Table of Contents

Map
Introduction
Chapter 1 Earliest Residents, Tour Stop #1
Chapter 2 Ghost of Annie Simpson
Chapter 3 Cedar Key Indian Burial Grounds, Tour Stop #2
Chapter 4 Headless Horseman of Cedar Key, Tour Stop #3
Chapter 5 Red Luck and the Ghost Ship, Tour Stop #4
Chapter 6 Seminoles, Timber and War! Tour Stop #5
Chapter 7 Ghost of the Headless Horse
Chapter 8 Wrath of the Civil War in Cedar Keys, Tour Stop #6
Chapter 9 A Wife in Chains
Chapter 10 Wailing Widow, Tour Stop #7
Chapter 11 The Cemeteries of Cedar Key
Chapter 12 A Thousand Mile Walk to Cedar Key, John Muir, American Legend, Tour Stop #8
Chapter 13 Post-Civil War Boom Years, Tour Stop #9
Chapter 14 Another Seahorse Ghost Story
Chapter 15 Boom to Bust, the 1896 Hurricane and the Ghost of a Railroad Man, Tour Stop #10
Chapter 16 Miss Susie, "Midwife of Cedar Key," Tour Stop #11
Chapter 17 Miss Bessie, Tour Stop #12
Chapter 18 Ghosts of the Island Hotel
Chapter 19 Arthur "Cush" Holston, Tour Stop #13
Chapter 20 The Ghosts of the Hale Building, Tour Stop #14
Chapter 21 Cedar Key Historical Society Museum, Tour Stop #15
Acknowledgments
Partial Bibliography

Debra Lyon-Dye

Cedar Key Spirit Tour

Map for Spirit/History Tour

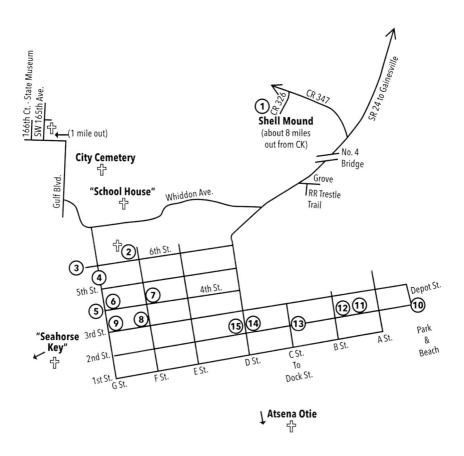

Circled numbers indicate 15 stops on the tour.
Cemeteries noted by ✣.
Specific directions in each chapter.
Distances on map not to scale.

Debra Lyon-Dye

Introduction

My Great Aunt Helen, a "spinster" school teacher, was the family historian. She told me, "Some people live with one foot in the past, and some with one foot in the future." Like her, I find exploring the past much more fascinating than the present or the future. I am proud to be an "old soul."

My personal history in Cedar Key began in the mid-1980s. My husband and I were married at the Island Hotel and bought a cottage on Fifth Street. Finally, in the 1990s, I secured a teaching position at the small, Pre K-12 school in Cedar Key and moved to the island full-time. Spit up and tossed out from the bilge of South Florida, I landed on the island a wide-eyed refugee. When one of my rough and tumble first graders brought in a collection of obviously authentic Indian weapons and tools made from hand crafted flint for Show and Tell, I knew this history buff had landed in the right spot.

For years I studied the history of the Cedar Keys, as it was once called, and started collecting ghost and spirit stories. I also learned about local folks who had become legends in the town. I read, researched, and took notes. I began the original Cedar Key Historic Spirit Tours in 2012. After much fact checking for accuracy and securing approval from the Cedar Key Museum's board, I led sunset walking and golf cart tours around Cedar Key. I told the history of the area in chronological order by retelling ghost stories and tales. For two years in my black cape and boots I led tours and collected even more local lore. It was fun and wildly successful, but the real purpose was to set it all down on paper to preserve and share.

So, walk with me around the Cedar Keys: a paradise for the history buff! I promise a most enlightening experience. The tour consists of 15 stops and all but the first one are in downtown Cedar Key. The second stop, beginning at the Indian Burial Grounds in Cedar Key, loops around town ending at the Historical Society Museum. This is an easy one mile walk or golf cart ride. Cedar Key is full of surprises, both historical and spiritual! Enjoy!

Debra Lyon-Dye

Cedar Key Spirit Tour

TOUR STOP 1
Chapter 1

Earliest Residents

Historic Spirit Tour Stop No. One: Shell Mound Park and Trail, eight miles north of Cedar Key on County Rd. 326, off Highway 347. (The only one of 15 tour stops outside the village of Cedar Key.)

We begin with a very brief summary of our earliest residents, then proceed to the 1700s and 1800s and our first ghost story. It is well worth the drive to Shell Mound Trail. I hope you find a quiet time to visit, so that you can reflect and take in all that once was here.

About 10,000 BC Paleo-Indians entered North Florida. These Indians were part of the great migration of people from Asia who crossed the then-passable Bering Strait to Alaska and then spread throughout the Western hemisphere.

At that time, during an Ice Age, sea levels were much lower, and the Florida peninsula was twice as large as it is today. The Gulf of Mexico shoreline was more than 100 miles west of where it is now and Florida was drier and cooler. Large animals such as bison, wooly mammoths, giant sloths and saber-toothed cats roamed vast grasslands. Extensive hunting by these nomadic Indians and eventual rising seas due to a global warming trend, led to the extinction of these big game animals. This was the Archaic Period from 8,000 BC to 750 BC.

Evidence in the form of bones, tools, and other artifacts found in shell mounds or middens confirm that 4-5,000 years ago, Archaic Indians began to settle along the coast of Cedar Keys and lived in the Shell Mound area. Adapting to rising seas and warmer weather they settled near the coast, depending more on marine and coastal animals. Raw chert, a flint-like stone, was used for tools and fired clay pottery was used for storing, preparing and serving food.

First, the Archaic, then Woodland Indians lived in the area for some 3,000 years, creating many mounds or middens up to 28 feet tall, like the mound at Shell Mound Historic Site, six miles north of Cedar Key, off Highway 347.

Shell Mound, at the end of County Road 326, covers about six acres and is the largest mound on the Central Gulf Coast. It is part of The Lower Suwannee National Wildlife Refuge. The Refuge is available for driving, hiking, biking, bird and wildlife watching, and studying. There is a small, county-managed campground just before the entrance to Shell Mound.

In March 2013, I first attended a lecture by Dr. Kenneth Sasserman, a University of Florida Professor of Florida Archeology. The lecture was sponsored by the Cedar Key Friends of the Library and was held at the Community Center on Sixth Street, not 100 feet from the town's Indian Burial ground. He has since returned many times to provide updates on his project.

Dr. Sasserman has been excavating the Shell Mound area since 2008. This includes 30 coastal miles of the refuge and some 13 islands. In 2009, with students, local residents and volunteers, Dr. Sasserman conducted a survey to learn about the Shell Mound area Indians' maritime way of life.

In his "Preliminary Report on Archeological Investigations at Shell Mound (8LV42, April 15, 2012)," he writes that Shell Mound is very true to its form when it was abandoned some 2,000 years ago. This period of maritime living was a time of adapting to coastal changes in an area that "continues to be diminished by rising seas." His team unearthed oyster shells, vertebrate fauna (mostly fish), shell tools, shards of Deptford period pottery from 2,500 years BP and organically enriched sand. (BP is a term used by archeologists for before present, or before 1950, a date often obtained through radio-carbon dating.)

Further excavating even deeper down into carefully dug sites at Shell Mound and nearby Deer and Bird Islands revealed materials dating to the "latter portion of the late Archaic Period, 4000-3500 BP." All items found were documented by depth, date, and sequence of activity. Deep pits containing shells (many with holes in them to extract the mollusk inside), stones, seeds, fish bones, and charcoal were found. He believes "the burning may have been ritual." Postholes, which have been located from 4,000 years ago, may help recreate the buildings, "probably villages with houses in circles around the center." Dr. Sasserman believes the U shaped shell ridge around the area was a storm break oriented toward the winter solstice. He hypothesizes that there were "at least three dozen mound villages, with 50 people in each village, Shell Mound being the community center."

"Measurements lead one to conclude that Shell Mound was constructed to model the islands of the Cedar Keys, a U shape facing west, sited on the setting sun of the winter solstice, similar to Stonehenge and Machu Picchu."

---Dr. Kenneth Sasserman

There are many theories as to why the Indians of Florida built mounds or middens: to stay above flood waters, to stay above biting insects, to be able to see strangers approaching, to see much sought-after game, simply to dump discarded food waste and broken tools, to elevate chiefs and religious leaders, to mark out public boundaries and plazas, and finally, to construct sites for ceremonial purposes and platforms for the dead. Due to the organic matter in these structures, they are usually darker than the soil around them, and vary from region to region.

Dr. Sasserman envisions a re-creation of the villages at Shell Mound based on his studies. He added that the Cedar Keys are littered with burial sites and from time to time bodies appear on eroding beaches. Hog Island, also known as Graveyard, Palmetto, Rattlesnake, and Pine Island, is a graveyard mound and is probably the biggest cemetery in the area, besides the sea. Hundreds of bodies in vessels and pots of bones have been badly looted despite laws which protect human remains. Dr. Sasserman hypothesizes that as sea levels rose, the indigenous people moved their dead inland and reburied them on platforms or middens of shells. He believes that the Indians left the coastal area about the year 800 A.D.

By the 1500s when the Spanish arrived, 350,000 aboriginal Floridians had settled into approximately 15 powerful chiefdoms or cultures which included the Timucua. The Weeden Island culture of north and northwest Florida was part of this large Timucuan-speaking society. As Hernando DeSoto moved north, he destroyed a Timucua village on Long

Pond in Chiefland, northeast of Cedar Key in the late 1500s. By the time Florida passed from the Spanish to the French, back to the Spanish, to the English (1763), and back to Spanish ownership, only a handful of indigenous people remained. Most were killed by warfare and European diseases to which they had no immunity: measles, small pox, and other infections. The rest scattered to points south in Florida or Cuba or were enslaved. A population of hundreds of thousands was decimated.

According to Jerry Wilkinson, www.keyshistory.org, in 1750, as whites became interested in the area, Creek Indians were driven west and also south to Florida, eventually mingling with other 'cimarrons' (Spanish for runaways or wild ones, which included former slaves) and became the Seminoles.

One of my favorite walks in addition to the 0.3 mile loop around Shell Mound is the adjacent one mile Dennis Creek Trail. Shell Mound is also the venue of our first ghost story, or should I say ghost stories, which involve the many sightings of poor Annie Simpson.

There is a bench on the Shell Mound trail that overlooks the Gulf of Mexico. As you sit there gazing at the Gulf, you will get the feeling that you are not alone. You will get the feeling that many from the past look over your shoulder with you. See if I am not right!

Chapter 2

The Ghost of Annie Simpson

"Las Islas Sabinas," (Spanish for The Islands of Cedar), were known to be a safe harbor. For thousands of years, the some thirteen islands provided a safe harbor and source of fresh water for Indians, Cuban sailors, British, French and Spanish traders, and PIRATES!

According to historian Toni Collins' book, *Cedar Key Light Station,* "Diaries of early explorers contain references to shacks, wells, and watch towers found on the various islands indicating that early sailors sought refuge on the islands when needed." The islands were surveyed by the British in the 1770s. In 1818 Alexander Arbuthnot, a British trader, set up an outpost at the mouth of the Suwannee River. There he traded with the Creek Indians, drifting down from the north. Timber cruisers first set their eyes on the islands' rich stands of cedar, cypress, and pine and would later return. From 1763 to 1783 the area was under British rule, then until 1813 the Spanish, and finally it became a U. S. Territory in 1821.

According to the Cedar Key Historical Society Museum's booklet, *Old Cedar Key Walking Tour,* traders included Renato Beluche, an associate of the Laffite brothers. A 2012 journal entry by J. L. Grummond notes that Beluche "scuttled more than a million dollars' worth of Spanish shipping in the Gulf of Mexico and Caribbean in two years." Since the 1500s, pirates had been commissioned by foreign governments to attack competing interests and acquire fortune along Florida's coastline, but they also looked out for their own self interests.

A University of Florida College of Education article published in 2002, "Exploring Florida," confirms that "Jean Lafitte, the pirate, visited Seahorse Key around 1800, using its high land as a lookout point." Although Jean Lafitte was a known smuggler, privateer and slave trader, he saw himself as an entrepreneur and defender of American freedom.

Annie Simpson:

Dangerous place, Cedar Keys, in the early 1800s. And so warned the parents of young and beautiful Annie Simpson, who lived in an isolated area just north of Cedar Key. Yet she strolled the woods and coastline of what we now know as Shell Mound, secure in the company of her giant wolf hound dog. Or so she thought. Usually wearing a black skirt and white blouse the young brunette of about 16 years strolled peacefully with her dog by her side. But one day, legend has it, she startled pirates burying treasure on a giant shell mound. They killed and buried both her and the dog, keeping them quiet forever. Her parents were devastated by her disappearance. It is said that a year or so after her death, a travelling psychic was begged by the family to help locate her. In a séance he heard Annie speak. "I have met death by violent means and only wish a proper burial." Her family searched and searched, but never found her body, or the dog's.

Sightings of the ghost of Annie Simpson, also known as the "Ghost Lady of Shell Mound," in and around Shell Mound have been numerous and continuous. Many have been published in books, magazines and newspapers. I begin with an account by Anna Rae Roberts published by M. A. Ralls from the *St. Petersburg Times Floridian,* Halloween of 1982. Anna Rae's account is also included in Joyce Elson Moore's *Haunt Hunter's Guide to Florida.*

Anna Rae was the wife of local artist, cowboy, fishing guide and now author Bill Roberts. But her story is from the 1960s and involves her first husband. She and her husband and another man harvested oysters out of the waters around Shell Mound and used an old '59 Chevy that they had taken the back seat out of. Filling the trunk and back seat with oysters they would then bring them to town to sell. One cold foggy January, as she waited for the two men to return, she sat in the car alone on the one lane road. She was facing the water waiting for the boat, but in the gloom noticed a white light coming down the road toward her. Nervously she rolled up the window. All she could see was the light, hovering some four feet off the ground. It kept its distance from the car, drifted by and then disappeared into the woods.

She retold what had happened to her a week or so later in town. A friend within earshot began crying and trembling and said she too had a bad experience near the same area. While camping and fishing with her husband she went into the woods heeding the call of nature. This time it was during a low tide and full moon. She was chased out of the woods by a figure in a long dress, hovering a full foot above the ground with a round light where her head should be, no arms nor legs.

Anna Rae and her husband stayed on Garden Island. She remembered one night when they were awakened by the barking of their dog. When they went out to investigate they saw the slight figure of a woman sitting on the bow of their 22 foot skiff. As she disappeared in the fog, they did not investigate!

Another story involves a family of three who were enjoying Shell Mound. The father went off to fish and the mother and her eight-year-old daughter set up a picnic. The child kept wandering farther and farther into the woods and her mother kept calling her back. Finally, the child said, "She wants me, Mommy," and began to disappear into the woods. Her mother grabbed her arm; and as she did, saw a woman in white leaning against a tree, beckoning to her daughter. The family immediately left but reported that as they left, they looked back and saw the woman and a very large dog at the edge of the trees.

A Mr. Faircloth, who lived near Shell Mound, is said to have seen the young lady when she walked up to his front porch. When he asked, "Can I help you, miss?" she dissolved into thin air. The second time this happened, he promptly moved away from Shell Mound to the safety of town.

In the 1970s a treasure hunter from St. Petersburg used a metal detector on the mound, and in the first few days found nothing but an old cistern and some other metal. But on the third day he found a corroded wood chest with metal bands, some coins, and…the skeleton of a very large dog.

On one of my tours one evening, a local woman told me about all the treasure hunting that had been done by locals at Shell Mound in years past. No treasure was ever found, but she did tell a chilling tale about a very deep and wide hole that emitted a foul blast of air. Some took to filling the hole with mattresses and trash to stop it up.

Annie Simpson has never been found, nor has she ever received the proper burial she desired. Yet she continues to walk often during a full moon, below and around the islands of Shell Mound, always disappearing in the mist and fog.

We move now to town!

Debra Lyon-Dye

TOUR STOP ② Chapter 3

Cedar Key Indian Burial Grounds

Historic Spirit Tour Stop No. Two: Burial Grounds, Sixth and F Streets, Cedar Key Community Center.

You are looking at an Indian Burial Site, maintained by the Garden Club of Cedar Key. **Please do not go on the mound.**

The mounds and middens of the current city of Cedar Key are also being studied by Dr. Sasserman. It is believed that the remains found in the 1960s in the mound at the Cedar Key Community Center at Sixth and F Streets in Cedar Key are the remains of Timucua Indians. Cedar Key, not unlike the rest of Florida, used the shells and "debris" found in mounds for building roads and houses, until they discovered their historical and sacred value. Many homes in the historic district of Cedar Key were built on mounds. There are many photos of these homes and mounds in the Cedar Key Historical Museum.

For more information on this time period and to see Indian artifacts, visit the Cedar Key Historical Museum at Second and D in Cedar Key; the Cedar Key Museum State Park, 12231 SW 166th Ct., Cedar Key; and The Florida Museum of Natural History, Gainesville, Florida. The Museum of Natural History is also, by the way, the best place to contact if you "find" any Indian weapons, tools, or artifacts on your property. Of course, it is now against the law to search for or collect any Native American artifacts on any Federal or state-owned or controlled land or waterway. Your "small find" is a piece of a window of time and even moving it forever alters the history it tells. It should go without saying, if you find human remains; call 911-- disturbing human remains is also illegal!

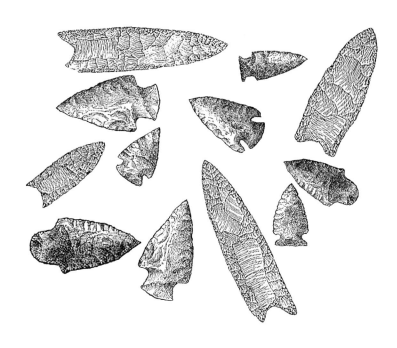

TOUR STOP ③

Chapter 4

The Ghost of the Headless Horseman of Seahorse Key

Historic Spirit Tour Stop No. Three: Sixth and G Streets, looking west.

Now travel west on Sixth Street, towards the bench with a view of Seahorse Key.

Admiring the sunset from Cedar Key, at Sixth and G, Seahorse Key is the island slightly to the left. Home to the oldest lighthouse still standing on the Gulf coast, a University of Florida Marine Studies lab, a sturdy dock, and a cemetery, it is also home to 600 to 1,000 cottonmouth snakes that thrive in a symbiotic relationship with the keys' nesting birds. But that is another story. (Note: In April of 2015 the nesting birds left the island and have yet to return. The snakes, left without bird droppings, are cannibalizing. The cause of the birds' sudden disappearance is yet to be discerned.)

For the tale of The Headless Horseman, we must return to the first decade of the 1800s when there was nothing on the island save for trees, sand, game, and an occasional visitor.

This account of the Headless Horseman is from a tiny book by Sally Tileston and Dottie Comfort called *Cedar Key Legends*. It is from a dog-eared copy I received from friend, Cedar Key native, teacher, historian and former co-worker Brenda Coulter. She dates it to the 1950s and I quote from its Foreword:

Men dedicated to the bitter struggle against the elements—changing tides, icy cold, blistering sun and hurricane winds—to catch fish, trap crabs and net turtles as a means of livelihood spend solitary hours on the Gulf. Thus there is time for musing. Many become natural philosophers.

Among these generations of seagoing men have arisen stories which, told and retold, become part of their background in this old fishing village.

In this booklet appear such tales handed down through the years. Most are based on reality, but enhanced by imagination. That these legends are believable or not is irrelevant, for they are the folklore of Cedar Key.

It is a fact that in the early 1800s Jean Lafitte traversed the waters between Cuba and other islands of the Caribbean, New Orleans and Galveston. It is probable that he often used the islands of Cedar Key as a stopping point, to trade, replenish provisions, or hide stolen goods. It is a fact that he frequented Seahorse Key, as it was the highest spot around from which to spot trouble, and half way between the locations in which he was the trouble!

During one of his missions to Louisiana he left a large treasure with his trusted henchman, Pierre Blanch (aka Le Blanch) on Seahorse Key. In addition to the treasure, which Pierre was to guard, Lafitte also left him with provisions and a beautiful Palomino; a fine horse from the stolen herd he was transporting north. He promised to return and left Pierre to guard and patrol the desolate island.

Pierre was marooned for many months, living off fish and game, only the horse to keep him company, until one day a visitor in a skiff approached the small island.

The visitor was Leon, a snake hunter, making his living off rattler and moccasin hides which brought a nice profit in those days. Leon befriended the island's only resident and the two enjoyed one another's company, both living rather solitary lives. But soon, the wiley Leon began to wonder why Pierre, having all the traits and characteristics of a pirate, was camped on the island.

Several nights he sailed silently to the south side of the island and spied on Pierre, finally catching him leaving his camp and walking along the shore about two hundred feet to a clump of palmettos. There he watched him kneel and dig into the sand until he unearthed two wooden chests of glittering coins. After checking the contents and muttering an oath to Lafitte, Pierre the pirate returned the chests to the ground, smoothed the sand back, and walked back to camp. Leon returned to his temporary home near the Cedar Keys and worked on a plan to steal the treasure.

A week or so later, Leon returned to his friend Pierre and this time brought not only food, but also a large quantity of good "corn licker" wrapped in burlap bags, something truly irresistible to the pirate. The two proceeded to make merry on the beach, Leon making sure the pirate drank far more than his share.

Cedar Key Spirit Tour

Well into the moonlit night, Pierre passed out, and Leon made his move down the beach to the treasure. He dug the heavy chests from beneath the palmetto bushes and was emptying their contents into the burlap bags when he noticed the shadow of the pirate looming over him.

Leon jumped up pulling out his razor sharp hunting knife to face Pierre, who was brandishing his gleaming curve-bladed cutlass. The two squared off and began circling until finally Pierre, who was on higher ground, swung the heavy cutlass at Leon. But Leon jumped back and then forward towards Pierre. His knife flashed up and then down Pierre's body and the pirate went down. In a fit of madness he grabbed the cutlass and with one slicing blow, severed the pirate's head and watched as it rolled on the sand.

Leon finished emptying the coins into the bags he had brought, and in a fit of meanness put the severed head in one of the chests. "There Lafitte, that's what you'll find when you return!"

But Lafitte did not return, his death or disappearance still a mystery. Nor did Leon return, having gotten away with murder and a pirate's treasure. But at low tide, along the sandy beaches of Seahorse Key, many sailors and fishermen have seen a headless figure astride a pale Palomino, keeping faithful patrol on a moonlit night.

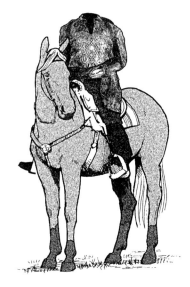

And that is the story of the Headless Horseman of Cedar Key!

Debra Lyon-Dye

TOUR STOP ④
Chapter 5

Red Luck and the Ghost Ship

From the 1600s-1800s the Gulf of Mexico was busy with pirates, and the legend of "Red Luck and his Ghost Ship" is a favorite of fishermen and other boaters who take their luck on the bountiful but dangerous waters. The legend is referenced in the *Rivers of America* series, under *The Suwannee, Strange Green Land*. McClelland's racy novel, *Tattoo Blues,* also refers to Red Luck. And most locals will never forget the meals prepared at Pat Hibbitt's long gone restaurant on the dock, "Pat's Red Luck," named after the pirate.

Historic Spirit Tour No. Four: Read this section as you walk south, downhill on G Street, towards the next bench or "pocket park" at Fourth Street.

Red Luck was a pirate and smuggler who frequented the western coast of Florida. One of his favorite stops was a trading post near the Suwannee River, where a wealthy Frenchman lived by the name of Monsieur Comte. While the two men were friends and enjoyed a lucrative trading business, the pirate also frequented Comte's plantation to visit and admire his beautiful, young daughter Laura Lou. As the two became closer, they were forced to hide their relationship from Laura Lou's father. They both knew that Monsieur Comte would not "cotton to" the idea of his daughter's spending her future with a pirate.

The time period has been narrowed down to the 1820s to early 1830s and more permanent residents were populating Way Key, as Cedar Key was then called. It is said that while trading in Way Key, Monsieur Comte got wind of the pirate's relationship with his daughter and vowed to his friends to kill the pirate. But the pirate was well liked in the area and some of his fisherman friends warned him of Comte's plans to kill him. So Red Luck and Laura Lou plotted to run away and sail for Cuba on the pirate's ship. But before leaving, Red Luck promised that he would someday, somehow repay the fishermen for saving his life and ensuring his happy future with Laura Lou.

So Red Luck and his future bride sailed south into the Gulf for Cuba. But a happy ending was not to be, as they sailed into the path of a hurricane and all aboard perished when the ship went down.

A year or so later--in fact this part of the story is repeated over and over in many ports along the Gulf coast--some Cedar Key fishermen were lost in one of the many dense winter fogs that silently slide over the landscape, fogs that sometimes last for brief periods of time, sometimes for weeks. Legend has it that the hapless fishermen floated off shore for two days, dropping sails and waiting, until on the third day, they spotted a large ship off the bow barely visible in the fog and decided to follow it. They figured they had nothing to lose as it was probably heading to shore or in any event could rescue them. They trailed the ship for some time until they saw the outline of Way Key and gave up a shout. As they turned to hail the ship that had guided them, it disappeared into the mist, never to be seen again.

That is until the next time a boat is hopelessly lost, and the ghost of a pirate and his ship, once again guides its crew to safety... to pay back a very old favor.

Debra Lyon-Dye

TOUR STOP 5
Chapter 6

Seminoles, Timber and War!

Historic Spirit Tour Stop No. Five: G and Fourth Streets.

Find the bench and sit a while, listening while you gaze at the waters of the Gulf.

As previously noted, Spain ceded Florida to the United States in 1821. The Cedar Keys, however, went mostly undiscovered until the mid-1830s when two timber cruisers made their way down the Suwannee River and then south to find islands covered with cedar, cypress, pine, other hardwoods, and a harbor for shipping.

Unfortunately, legislators, settlers, and business leaders found themselves in yet another war with Indian tribes who resented more and more settlers encroaching on their lands. The Second Seminole Indian War, 1835-42, would have a great influence on Cedar Keys; the timber riches would have to wait for later.

Due to the conflict, it was determined by General, later to be president, Zachary Taylor, who in 1839 personally visited the islands of Cedar Key, that they be reserved for "military purposes." What is now known as Atsena Otie, Creek Indian for Cedar Island, became home to a hospital, supply depot, and army headquarters, thus, Depot Key. Nearby Seahorse Key would also become an army post with Indian internment camp and cemetery. A post was also established at Fort No. 4 near the present day No. 4 Bridge.

The Seminole internment camps held and transferred men, women, and children who were being forcibly sent west. Indians who tried to escape relocation camps in Tampa were sent in chains to Seahorse Key.

Finally, the Seminole Chieftains surrendered and according to historian Toni Collins in her book *Cedar Keys Light Station*, "On August 1842, by Order No. 28 issued at the Cedar Keys, Colonel Worth announced hostilities with the Indians within the Territory of Florida had ceased..." Strangely, as preparations were made to abandon the post, a great hurricane struck destroying most of the buildings on the Cedar Keys. There has been some reference to an Indian curse; an omen of misfortune from the Great Spirit.

In 1842, The Florida Armed Occupation Act was enacted. It declared that a Florida resident could apply by permit and be granted 160 acres of land if they built a house on the property the first year, cleared and cultivated five acres, and remained on the property for five years. Naturally, they would have to deal with any remaining Indians, who were banished to the south of Florida.

Permitting began in earnest. A Mr. Thomas Parsons made application for Way Key, currently the town of Cedar Key. Samuel Johnson received a permit for Seahorse Key, later to be involved in a court fight as the property was still held by the military. Mr. Augustus Steele requested a permit for Depot Key, renamed Atsena Otie. Mr. Steele managed to be the only bidder at an auction and acquired all the structures and materials left by the military for a mere $227. Mr. Steele was also a close friend of Florida Senator, David Levy Yulee, a man with a dream of a railroad and the namesake of our county.

Mr. Steele and Mr. Levy also dreamed about the Cedar Keys becoming a port due to the maritime travel from the eastern United States and the islands of the Caribbean around Florida's west coast on to New Orleans and Texas and points west. Finally, after much petitioning, a lighthouse was established on Seahorse Key in 1854.

Army Engineer Lt. George Meade of Civil War fame constructed the light station on the island's 45 foot hill with a work party from Philadelphia. Again referring to historian Toni Collins, the "light was 75 feet above sea level and visible 15 miles out into the Gulf of Mexico."

The next year, Yulee's dream of a railroad from Fernandina to Cedar Key was also finally coming to fruition. Yulee's Florida Railroad Company had secured a U. S. Government mail contract to get the U. S. mail from Charleston, South Carolina to New Orleans in sixty hours, as opposed to the several weeks it was taking. Time saved is money earned, and the economic benefits of a cross state railroad were huge. Building a twelve-foot-high track across hurricane-prone Florida with slave labor was no easy task, however, and the train did not roll in to Cedar Key until March 16, 1861. Eleven years of toil and trouble, to be met with the greatest of toil and trouble. But, remain seated, it is time in our history for another ghost story!

Chapter 7

The Ghost of the Headless Horse

There were twelve light keepers who kept the Fresnel lens operating on Seahorse Key. They did not stay very long on the lonely island, where pay was sporadic, rations irregular, and the three mile boat trip to town risky. One of them was referred to as Old Man Gardner, who according to local lore, incurred problems of a different sort.

Old Man Gardner and his wife lived on Seahorse Key with their lovely young daughter. One day, on an infrequent trip to Way Key, the girl met and fell in love with a Yankee flagman, a railroad man. Her parents were quite unaware of the relationship. The two had plans to marry until someone, either in sympathy or mischief, revealed to the girl that the Yankee was already married to a wife up north. When she went to confront her lover, he had disappeared, never to be seen again.

The disconsolate girl took to staying at home with her parents on Seahorse Key, never travelling to Way Key or the mainland. She roamed the island in a cloud of sadness. Her parents soon learned the source of her broken heart and were at first angry and then deeply concerned. Finally, after months of her moping around the island, Old Man Gardner procured a beautiful white horse to keep his daughter company and hopefully cheer her.

The beautiful heartbroken girl rode the beaches of Seahorse Key on the horse, but wished only to die. Finally, she took her life in the kitchen of the lighthouse. (Her blood stain marked the spot for many years, until a marine paint was found to finally cover it.) Her parents naturally were distraught and mourned her daily. The horse, now without its rider, did not help as he wandered, head down, looking for his mistress. The horse was a constant reminder of their dead daughter and one day in a fit of madness, the old man attacked the horse with his machete, severing its head. It is said that after, he sat on his knees and rocked the head for hours, wailing as he did so.

The parents soon left the island in their misery and moved far away. But, many a fisherman and sailor on a moonlit night at low tide, have seen the shadow of a headless horse wandering the sands of Seahorse Key. Thus, the Ghost of the Headless Horse of Seahorse Key lives on.

It should be noted here, that this is Cedar Key native and author P. H. Day's rendition, "as told to him by Sammy Lindsey." Also, according to historian Toni Collins, there were two light keepers by the name of Gardner, and that while records indicate no children, she has seen a photo of one of the Gardner families at the lighthouse, with a grown girl standing between her parents.

Cedar Key Spirit Tour

TOUR STOP 6
Chapter 8

The Wrath of the Civil War in Cedar Keys

Historic Spirit Tour Stop No. Six: The Oldest House in Cedar Key, the "Block House" at G and Fourth Streets.

We leave Seahorse Key, for now, and move to the corner of G and Fourth. There, now painted pink, stands the oldest house in Cedar Key, the old "Block House." So named because in 1920 its coquina exterior was scored with lines, giving the 1860 façade the appearance of being built of blocks. We use this venue because this lovely two-story home was witness to the Civil War and still stands to tell a story.

History has brought us to 1860. Senator David Levy Yulee has secured a government contract to get the mail from Charleston to New Orleans in sixty hours. After eleven long years of toil and trouble he delivers on his promise to cross Florida with a railroad, and on March 16, 1861, his steam train *Abner McGehee* arrives in Cedar Key from Fernandina Beach with the mail. The U. S. Mail ship Atlantic is waiting in Cedar Keys' harbor to receive the mail. There is one problem, however. Less than two months earlier, Florida had been the third state to secede from the Union and Senator Yulee had led a delegation of senators to withdraw from the Union. He, in fact, had left Washington, D. C., for Fernandina. His mail contract with the Union was now null and void. The mail went on its way, but Senator Yulee lost out on a very lucrative contract. He now feared for his reportedly blockaded railroad terminus in Fernandina, just north of Jacksonville, and made plans to secure both home and fortune.

It should be noted here that as you drive into Cedar Key on Hwy. 24, you can look to the left and see the elevated berm of the tracks running parallel to the road. As you cross no. 4 Bridge you can see a series of islands also to your left which brought the tracks to Way Key. You can walk a section of the tracks on the Trestle Trail on Grove Street and then find it again in the Nature's Landing Condominium complex by the dock. The portion of the railroad depot that is left is now the blue Nature's Landing Office building. The tracks continued out onto Dock St., with a spur on the beach so that after deliveries, the train could back up and then return to the mainland. There is an excellent rendition of this in the "1884 Birdseye Map of Cedar Key" hanging over the books for sale at the Cedar Key Historical Museum.

Back to 1860. The census indicates that there were 214 people living on Atsena Otie and 161 on Way Key. As word reached Cedar Key about secession and trouble with the Yankees, local militias were formed and blockade runners organized, but eventually most Cedar Keyans responded by leaving. When the war actually struck the area, fewer than 100 people lived on the two keys.

In preparation for the unpleasantness, Lighthouse Keeper Malloy, who some suspected as disloyal, was let go and a company of the 4th Florida Infantry took up duties on Seahorse Key. The local townspeople removed the valuable lens, and according to historian and author Toni Collins, shipped the lens, one can of oil, an empty oil can, and one pump to Waldo for safekeeping, all for $5.70.

Robert E. Lee visited and surveyed Florida in 1861. He recommended to Jefferson Davis that the Confederate States of America not try to defend Florida's 1,400 miles of coastline, but rather the rich agricultural resources of its interior. It was reasoned that the coast would be impenetrable to the Union. In fact, the Confederate forces on Seahorse Key were reduced to one lieutenant and 22 men. According to noted Historian Charles C. F. Fishburne, Jr., "Confederate Brigadier General J. H. Trapier, Commander in E. Florida, made sure the record showed that he had moved the defenders from Cedar Keys to Fernandina in compliance with orders from his superior."

However, the first railroad terminus to come under attack in Florida was Cedar Key. In January of 1862 the *U.S.S. Hatteras* sailed into the nearly deserted Cedar Keys and as ordered "captured or destroyed all public property" on Way Key and Depot Key/Atsena Otie. Destroyed were ships containing cotton and turpentine, the railroad depot, seven freight cars, turpentine warehouses, and telegraph lines. Four schooners, three sloops, a ferryboat, a small sailboat and a launch were all seized. Only the "Schooner Fanny" survived. After shelling the port the Union took command of the Cedar Keys and rendered useless the military stores left on Seahorse Key, including, again according to Fishburne, "two eighteen-pounder cannons, their carriages, stores of ammunition, and the barracks." They discovered, however, that the valuable lighthouse lens was gone.

When news reached David Levy Yulee in Fernandina, he was furious. Two months later, the Union attack he had been anticipating struck Fernandina. He ordered all trains to head west, toward Baldwin, burning bridges behind them. In fact he was on the last car of the last train as the port was being shelled. His car was shelled and caught fire, several men killed or injured in the process. In flames, the car was disengaged from the train and Yulee himself jumped into the water, using a boat for his final trip to safety. Yulee retreated to his 5,100 acre sugar plantation "The Margarita" on the Homosassa River. There he and his family prospered running a very successful blockade operation, complete with companies of paid infantry. (According to a quote from historian Charles Tebeau, for just three of Yulee's "adventures to Cuba he was paid $3,939.99 in two months for an investment of $1,433.00 by the Confederate government.") Later in the war the Yulee family was captured, imprisoned in Savannah, and after the war released to return home.

There is an old story that in the process of sending the remains of the Confederate treasury by rail to Yulee's plantation for safe keeping, Federal troops caught up with the train, but found it empty of funds. There was much speculation as to its whereabouts.

Meanwhile, the occupied Cedar Keys became a Federal Military Post and a "rigid blockade" was set up. Union officers appropriated and occupied the Parson & Hale General Store, now the Island Hotel, on Second Street. War would not be kind to Cedar Key, but war is kind to only a select few. Augustus Steele, founder of Depot Key, and his wife relocated to Gainesville. (They never returned to the Cedar Keys, but Steele remained Customs Inspector, complete with income, until his death in 1864.) Those few Cedar Keyans who remained were at the mercy of the military, deserters, and marauders.

The Crevasse family name comes up frequently in this narrative and again according to historian Fishburne in his *The Cedar Keys in the Civil War* and *Reconstruction, 1861-1876,* Captain Joseph Napoleon Crevasse of Depot Key was a "skilled seaman and daring blockade-runner." Captain Crevasse, his son Joseph, and step-son Robert Clark, sailed the fifty-foot sloop "Minnie," running sugar and salt from the Homosassa sugar plantations, including Yulee's "Margarita," to camp Four at the No. Four Bridge. Outwitting the Union several times, including being let go after capture, they did "heroic work for the Confederacy" until capture in 1863. They returned, ill from imprisonment, to Cedar Key after the war.

One of the greatest needs of the war was salt: salt to preserve food, salt to cure leather, salt for livestock, and salt to fix dyes in uniforms. Due to the effective Union blockade, the south was in great need of salt. The camp at No. Four Bridge (Railroad Station No. 4) had a sizeable salt works. Salt water was boiled in giant kettles, the location chosen for the water's high concentration of salt due to a drought. According to historian Toni Collins, "Anyone engaged in making salt was exempt from military service so the salt making industry had little trouble finding workers." The No. Four camp, known since Seminole Indian War days, was located at Ludlow or Lutterloh's Ditch.

In 1862 the Union decided to attack and capture the South's remaining salt works. One of the first targeted salt works was that on the edge of Cedar Keys, No. 4 camp. While there is much local lore about the Battle at Lutterloh's Ditch, I again rely on Mr. Fishburne. There is also a wonderful diorama at the State Museum in Cedar Key on S. W. 166th Court illustrating the battle.

On October 4, 1862 the gunboat *U. S. S. Somerset* got as close to the salt works as they dared and began shelling. Then Lieutenant Commander English, ordered men ashore in small boats to "destroy all the salt works that could be found." When they came upon a large camp run by women who had hoisted a white flag, they stopped firing. As they disembarked, however, they were fired upon by men beyond the tree line and retreated to the *Somerset,* as the tide was ebbing.

Later that same day Commander Howell arrived on the gunboat *U.S.S. Tahoma.* He and a Lt. Crossman, joined English's troop and two days later the *Tahoma,* with 111 men, eight additional boats, two with howitzers, charged on the salt works. They destroyed the salt works, houses, 50 to 60 wrought iron and cast iron boilers, and outbuildings. The capacity of the works had been determined to be 150 bushels of salt a day.

Commander Howell reported to Admiral Lardner, "The rebels here needed a lesson and they have had it."

On February 13, 1865 a second and final battle occurred at Number Four. "Captain Ludlow whipped the Yankee troops and left their corpses strewn about the marsh." So go local claims.

In reality, a Federal post was established at No. Four Camp. Historian Fishburne documents that The Federal Second Florida Cavalry Regiment was headquartered there as well as "some troops of the Second Regiment U. S. Colored Infantry."

In February, a Major Edmund C. Weeks led some 386 Union soldiers from the camp to Levyville and Clay Landing, just north of here. The "enemy at the camp was surprised but not captured" according to Weeks. As they left for their home camp at No. Four, the rear guard was attacked by Confederate Captain John J. Dickison. Captain Dickison followed the Union troops back to Camp Four with 145 men, including 18 Florida militiamen under Captain Lutterloh. Major Weeks and his Union forces returned safely to Camp Four with "100 head of cattle, several wagons, 50 former Negro slaves, 13 horses, and 5 prisoners."

Both sides agree that shooting started at 7 a.m. on Monday, February 13. However, Major Weeks was on Depot Key, having left in charge Captain E. Pease, 2nd U. S. Colored Infantry, with only 40 men. In making his way back to Camp Four, a battle ensued on the bridge. Major Weeks claimed that, with his men, he took the bridge and made it to the camp, the Confederates retreating east for the night. A scout reported that they were some six miles out "near Yearty's place," regrouping with reinforcements and heading back northwest to the No. Four Camp. Major Weeks claims he did not want a night attack and so ordered his men back to Way Key.

Confederate Captain John Dickison had a different account. He reported a three and a half hour battle whereby he and his troops, outnumbered five to one, and running out of ammunition, drove the enemy back to Cedar Key with the loss of only five men wounded, none mortally; killing, wounding and capturing about 70 of the enemy and recapturing all cattle, horses, and wagons, "all of which were returned to their rightful owners." He writes, "The enemy was defeated at all points." He notes that had reinforcements not arrived to help the Union soldiers in the midst of battle and had his men not run out of ammunition, he would have "slaughtered them all."

But, fate was to strike Cedar Key once again as it was chosen to be the first leg of a broad plan to march on Florida to take Tallahassee, the only capital of the south not yet captured. Union reinforcements just happened along at the right time in the right place to assist Major Weeks. Their march on and capture of Tallahassee, however, was aborted as word spread that General Lee had surrendered to Grant at Appomattox, Virginia on April 9th, 1865.

Of note, on April 1st, Florida's Governor John Milton had committed suicide at his plantation "The Sylvania" in Marianna, Florida leaving Tallahassee with the message, "death would be preferable to reunion."

According to Fishburne, "it was becoming clear, reluctantly, to most that the Confederacy had lost the war. By May 20, the Confederate Stars and Bars no longer flew over the Florida Statehouse."

"Cedar Key was considered a **death-hole**..." according to Collins' *Cedar Keys Light Station,* as early as 1862. Seahorse Key was used to house prisoners and Atsena Otie was once again used as a supply depot and military hospital for troops. In Richard Edling's *Civil War Album,* he writes that the Union "invaded the town and burned down almost every building that wasn't needed to quarter troops or store supplies." You had, then, in very overcrowded and unsanitary conditions on Atsena Otie and Seahorse Key, women and children needing care while the men of the family were serving in the military or dead. There also were wounded soldiers carrying contagious diseases, former slaves, deserters, and other refugees of the war. That would be some 1,200 people on the two islands. By the end of the war, conditions, again quoting Collins, "...killed four to six, and sometimes nine to twelve people a day from typhoid, diarrhea, and fever."

If you have not yet visited the small cemeteries on Seahorse Key or Atsena Otie, suffice it to say that they were not buried there. Where were so many poor souls buried?

I leave you with this information found in *Transactions of the Medical Association of the State of Alabama* available on-line as an eBook. In the Appendix of Medical Papers, "Sketches of Yellow Fever on the Gulf Coast of Florida," dated 1879, there is this account:

Cedar Keys is the Gulf terminus of the railroad running from Fernandina across the state of Florida. It (Way Key) was a small village of about 20 houses before the war, of which all but one was burned down after the war commenced. During the war the place was deserted and was used as a burial ground for a refugee camp which was located on the neighboring keys of Atsena Otie, distant about two miles. In this way it is said that 1,200 dead bodies were buried beneath the soil upon which the town is built.

Now if I may editorialize here, given that according to author Toni Collins the entire population was 1,200, there is some speculation as to the number. Regarding Way Key used as a burial ground, while building a town on a burial ground was not uncommon in ancient Europe, it is more probable that the dead were buried at sea.

Time for a ghost story!

Chapter 9

A Wife in Chains

We began our Civil War chapter with the "Old Block House," and we need to remain there a little while longer. Built into the side of an Indian mound, as pictures at the Historical Society Museum show, the two story structure has seen much history and had many owners.

At some point in the late 1800s, the home, located at F and Fourth Streets, was inhabited by a man and his wife who had less than a harmonious relationship. It is said that the man discovered, or at least surmised, that the wife had been unfaithful to him. After a time she was never seen again, but neighbors believed that she was locked and possibly chained in the house. She was, in fact, never seen by anyone ever again. The man continued to live in the house for some time, but eventually died.

The home was neglected and abandoned, even used for a while as a chicken coup. This went on for many years. The windows of the house were broken by children and the house sat eerily empty except for occasional sounds. Late at night the sounds of rattling and clinking chains could be heard by its closest neighbors.

This story was told to me by a descendant of the Wilson family, that being Light Keeper William Wilson. She says that her grandmother, Mary Wilson, used to tell the story and warned the children not to go near the house, that "something terrible had happened there and that the poor woman's rattling chains could still be heard at night." Needless to say, the children all gave the house a wide berth especially at night when having

Cedar Key Spirit Tour

to go up to the "school house" for evening events. They would either go to the beach and walk up towards the school or head towards D Street and around, but most certainly avoid the house where "the lady rattled her chains."

The current owner, a friend, happily reports that this is just an old story and that he has never heard or seen a thing unusual in his abode.

Debra Lyon-Dye

TOUR STOP ⑦
Chapter 10
The Wailing Widow

Historic Spirit Tour Stop No. Seven: Fourth and F Streets.

Leaving the "Block House" at the corners of G and Fourth, stroll east with me to the next corner which is F Street. We stop here to admire the tall Hale-Johnson House with the widow's walk on top. The widow's walk enjoys an almost 360 degree view of the water. The home was built in 1870 in the Italianate Revival style but has been extensively remodeled, the second floor and widow's walk a newer addition. However, it provides the perfect vantage point for our next story, The Wailing Widow.

This story has already become obscure in Cedar Key. It is one of the five tales told in Sally Tileston and Dottie Comfort's "Cedar Key Legends." The tattered, typewritten fifteen-page book I have is a treasured copy I received from Cedar Key native Brenda Coulter. My version is much abbreviated. On my *Cedar Key Historic Spirit Tours* I told the story from the Hale-Johnson House to take advantage of the sight of the widow's walk. The original house of the widow was destroyed in one of Cedar Key's hurricanes and was in an entirely different location, believed to have been closer to the water.

Cedar Key has its fair share of tropical storms and hurricanes and you quickly recognize the signs, which are often more accurate than the media. If you see fiddler crabs crawling up and into your house to reach a higher vantage point, beware. If seagulls begin to line up on the high point of a street or airport runway, beware. If other birds head east to the mainland to wait it out, prepare. If snakes and turtles and raccoons begin moving to higher ground, watch out. Many of us have aches and pains which also signal a weather disturbance and then, of course, are the grey skies, winds, slow swells of water and unusual tides.

Back in the day, fishermen had to rely on these signs and make a judgement call. Which is exactly what happened to Amos Beasley and his fellow fishermen many years ago.

Amos' wife, Beattrice, was 'from inland' and feared for her husband more than the other Cedar Key wives. She never relaxed when he was out on the Gulf, probably with good reason. Amos was also a bit more daring than the others and often went out further than the rest of the fleet. So, one day when the waters appeared ominous, the men met in town to discuss whether to risk going out or miss an entire day of profitable fishing. The question was not if a hurricane was approaching, but when. No intermittent squalls of rain had begun. The men who advised that there was no danger for at least a whole day won the dispute. The white sails of the fleet lagged over the island. Beattrice took her usual place, on the widow's walk with its expansive view, to wait and watch.

Beattrice paced the widow's walk for hours in the increasingly worse conditions. The fishing fleet beat a hasty retreat in the face of the storm and sheltered in the protected lagoons of the islands. Quoting from the tattered book, "Half-crazed, Beatrice clung to the railing. In the darkness and lashing squalls she could not see if Amos' schooner had come back." Wind and rain pulled at Beattrice but she clung to the iron railing all night, bent against the wind, praying for Amos' return. "Neighbors tried to loosen her hold on the iron bars' in vain. She did not feel their hands as she shook them off. Her prayers began to be a banshees' wail, so high keyed it merged with the howl of the wind." All through the night she waited, but "at dawn, Amos' boat was missing."

Beattrice's neighbors brought her downstairs, but again and again she returned to the widow's walk searching the horizon for Amos. She was sure he had found shelter on one of the keys and would soon return to her. But Amos never did come home to Beattrice, and "for the rest of her life she refused to believe that her husband would never return."

The final paragraphs of the little story read:

Whenever a hurricane was rumored to be on its way, Beattrice would climb to her "Widow's Walk." She paced up and down, wrung her hands, sobbed until her lament resembled the screech of the winds in a wild storm. The citizens of Cedar Key came to believe her vigils proclaimed the approach of a storm.

After a hundred years, if anyone passes by the house with the "Widow's Walk" and hears a high-pitched keening he can think it is Beattrice's warning about a hurricane roaring on its way to Cedar Key.

As previously mentioned, although I have used the Hale-Johnson House as the site from which to frame this story, Beattrice's house is believed to have been blown down in a subsequent hurricane.

Chapter 11

The Cemeteries of Cedar Key

Before we continue with our walk through history, the days of Marshall Law, the return of the railroad, John Muir's walk and post-Civil War Cedar Key, we should pause and learn about the cemeteries. We owe much of our information about day-to-day life on the islands in that time thanks to school teacher Eliza Hearn. Her diary, at the Historical Society Museum, paints for us many details and we will be talking about her in length. So, let's start with her burial place, the first of six which you can later visit at your leisure.

The Hearn Cemetery:

Very few school campuses have on their grounds a cemetery, but Cedar Key School at the top of D and G Streets does.

Debra Lyon-Dye

If when facing the school you walk to the right along the sidewalk, past the playground you will see the gymnasium. If you stand in the parking lot you will see a small brick wall sheltering three graves, nearly forgotten until the 1980s when school teachers Brenda Coulter, Sally Baylor, and their 4-H Club members added the brick surround and grave marker.

Buried here are Captain Thomas Hearn and his two daughters, Eliza and her younger sister Amelia. Captain Hearn, widowed, brought his two daughters to Gainesville before the Civil War from Georgia, where he suffered business losses. A veteran of the Seminole Wars, he brought them up "in the faire of the Lord." Due to declining health he sought a change of climate and moved his daughters to Way/Cedar Key in the late 1850s. They homesteaded 80 acres of land at the present school site, taught and "cared for orphans" until the Civil War, when they left Cedar Key, as did most of its populace.

After the war, when the railroad returned, due to the efforts of David Levy Yulee and Confederate Captain Edward J. Lutterloh, the Hearns returned to their homestead and tried to make a living farming and teaching school. However, shortly after their return Captain Hearn died of cholera on September 10, 1866. The sisters trudged on through difficult years, including a rattlesnake bite which Eliza survived in 1869, until Amelia died in 1885, leaving her sister alone to survive on the island. Eliza continued to teach, sell vegetables from her garden, and try to make ends meet, thwarting the efforts of the powerful Captain Lutterloh, now Tax Accessor, and his Florida Town Improvement Company, the real estate arm of his and Yulee's Florida Railroad to tax and seize her property. She died on September 5, 1910, leaving no will, probably approaching seventy.

Local lore has it that she and her family donated their homestead to the school, but historian Fishburne details that it was probably seized by the local taxing authorities, thus becoming city property. It remains their final resting place.

Cedar Key Spirit Tour

City Cemetery, Gulf Blvd., Established 1886:

The City Cemetery, deeded to the city by the Florida Town Improvement Co. has approximately 750 graves in the main section, 24 in the "colored" section, and several below toward the water in a small Catholic section. The earliest marked grave is that of Leon Mallard, born 1802, died September 19, 1855, Lot 151. This shows that the cemetery was being used before the city had control of the property. Spaces used to be free but in 2015 cost $400 and are restricted in size to four foot by eight. A Board of Trustees handles cemetery sales and business. In earlier days the cemetery could only be reached at low tide. The anchor at the entrance was found by a Greek fisherman and later donated. Recently a board walk has been built at the water's edge around the cemetery and offers a very peaceful path. One of the more unusual stories from this site is about the man who wanted to be buried with his dog. So, when he died, his dog was shot as per his instructions, and buried with his master. (I was told the dog was old.)

Debra Lyon-Dye

The Bishop Family Cemetery on SW 165th Avenue (Private):

This Rye Key family cemetery, sometimes referred to as Bishop Point, dates from 1896. Four of the six graves are infants, one a toddler, and one Amanda Bishop, wife. This cemetery is on private property; the area at one time was a dairy.

Seahorse Key Cemetery:

As part of the Cedar Keys National Wildlife Refuge, the Seahorse Key Cemetery is only accessible at certain times of the year. When walking, do mind the island's famous water moccasins. The cemetery, 200 yards east of the lighthouse contains eight marked graves and many surrounding unmarked. Considering that hundreds of Seminoles were interred, transferred, and hospitalized on Seahorse Key and Atsena Otie, it can be assumed that there are numerous unmarked graves. The first known burial is that of Civil War U. S. gunboat *Tahoma* Assistant Paymaster James S. Turnbull, who died February 6, 1862. However, Turnbull's body was later moved to New York. The original marker of one Civil War casualty, Patrick Doran, a rope maker from New York, is on display at the Cedar Key Historical Society Museum. The cemetery contains the remains of three other Union soldiers; lighthouse keeper Wilson; the only female lighthouse keeper, Catherine Hobday, buried in 1879 at the age of 83; and two fishermen, one a blockade runner.

Seahorse Key Cemetery

Atsena Otie Cemetery:

The cemetery at Atsena Otie is located at the end of a walk down the former town's center as you leave the current dock. It is well marked, an easy walk, and best to do when cold, due to the island's ravenous mosquitoes. The original ornate iron fences are intact, along with beautiful old tombstones. The cemetery contains 28 gravesites, the earliest being 1877 and the latest 1910. Work was done on the cemetery by the Historical Society Museum in the summer of 2013 to keep the site clear of undergrowth.

Debra Lyon-Dye

Atsena Otie Cemetery

Atsena Otie Cemetery

Indian Burial Grounds:

Information was provided in Chapter Three on this site, located at 6th and F Streets.

An excellent resource for information on the cemeteries of Cedar Keys is historian Lindon Lindsey's 1994 publication, *Cemeteries of Levy and Other Counties.* The volume is available at the Historical Society Museum.

Debra Lyon-Dye

TOUR STOP 8
Chapter 12

A Thousand Mile Walk to Cedar Key, John Muir, American Legend

Historic Spirit Tour Stop No. Eight: Read and stroll south on F towards Third Street, (rest at bench).

While Eliza and Amelia Hearn struggled to put their daily bread on the table, John Muir walked in on what was left of the railroad lines on a warm October day in 1867, two years after the Civil War, and was stunned by the "sea air" and beauty of the island. The contrast in their observances of the time is much as it is today, when happy, smiling island visitors walk the same streets as working residents who strive to make a living on fickle seas and a five month tourist season.

Cedar Key Spirit Tour

John Muir, who in his later years founded the Sierra Club in 1892, is considered the Father of National Parks, and was lauded by presidents. But in 1867 a young Muir ended a 1,000 mile walk from his home in Indiana to Cedar Key, formulating his ideas of preserving the wilderness along the way. In the Cedar Key Historical Society Museum, there is a Muir display but as a docent there, the most frequent question I received was, "Why did he end his walk in Cedar Key?" Why, indeed!

Muir left Indianapolis, Indiana in October of 1867 and at the age of 29 walked south some 1,000 miles, walking up to 40 miles a day, with little to nothing to eat. He arrived on the Gulf Coast in December of that same year. He kept a leather-bound journal which he later edited and first published in the Overland Monthly and later as a beautifully written book, A Thousand Mile Walk to the Gulf in 1916.

Muir was a botanist and so interested in plants that it is written he "studied the sidewalks of Chicago for them." He was a gifted factory mechanic, but long dreamed of "the gardens of the south," and after an accident to his eyes, he set out on his journey, grateful that his injury was not permanent and wrote:

I have daily consulted maps in locating a route through the Southern states, the West Indies, South America, and Europe—a botanical journey I have studied for years. For many a year I have been impelled towards the Lord's tropic gardens of the South. I bade adieu to mechanical inventions, determined to devote the rest of my life to the study of the inventions of God...anywhere in the wilderness southward...if possible...into South America to see tropical vegetation in all its palmy glory.

Muir, plant press in hand, had already hiked and explored the Great Lakes region including Wisconsin, parts of Canada, Indiana, and Illinois. He set off with little money, a knife, his plant press and a compass for the South, "living off the kindness of the poorest of strangers." He detailed every plant species he encountered and collected specimens. From Indiana he walked through Kentucky and then through the Blue Ridge Mountains of Tennessee and northern Georgia. He commented that Athens, Georgia, was the one city that he wished later to revisit, it being the most beautiful. Warned to watch for rattlesnakes and following his compass to Savannah, he declared the people of Georgia the friendliest. He saw the scars of war on the land and its people.

The traces of war are not only apparent on the broken fields, burnt fences, mills and woods ruthlessly slaughtered, but also on the countenance of the people.

He arrived in Savannah on October 8, noting the numerous Magnolia grandiflora, and immediately set off for the post office where he was to have money wired from his brother. But no money arrived and for a week he camped in the Bonaventure Cemetery, a "grand forest of a graveyard."

The ideal place for a penniless wanderer, there no superstitious prowling mischief maker dare venture.

There he camped until his money finally arrived and on October 15 he set off for Florida on the steamship Sylvan, bound for the "rickety town of Fernandina" where he and his shipmates were set down without breakfast. He wandered for a while into the woods and swamps, not the "Land of Flowers" he envisioned, his biggest fear being alligators, especially when he slept. He once felt the presence of one behind him and heard the grasses rustle, "waiting only to be eaten," to turn and discover instead a "tall white crane." He wrote that in his travels, he never saw "more than one." He did not carry a pistol, but once in Florida he had to put his hand to his pistol pocket as a threat, which was effective.

Marveling at twenty-foot palms, "princes of the vegetable world," he stumbled about "in the trackless woods" until he found the remains of the railroad right-of-way and some logging trails. He headed off in the general direction of

Gainesville, which upon finding just three days later he described as "rather attractive—an oasis in the desert." He stayed there for a few days hunting for sport with an ex-judge and former Confederate Captain. His October 22nd entry describing a hunt with the two gentlemen reveals much. He reverses the role of man and beast showing the consciousness raising of a soon-to-be conservationist.

The captain and the judge, and myself stood at different stations where the deer was expected to pass, while a brother of the captain entered the woods to arouse the game from cover. The...deer...took a direction different from any which this particular old buck had ever been known to take in times past, and in doing so was cordially cursed as being the "d—dest deer that ever ran unshot." To me it appeared as "d—dest" work to slaughter God's cattle for sport. "They were made for us," say these self-approving preachers; "for our food, our recreation, or other uses not yet discovered." (But...) As truthfully we might say on behalf of a bear, when he deals successfully with an unfortunate hunter, "Men and other bipeds were made for bears, and thanks be to God for claws and teeth so long.

Muir headed for the Gulf coast, hoping to catch transport to Cuba and South America. Any local hiker or gardener can appreciate his account of slashing through the "tough vine-tangles" of Smilax, walking hot dusty sand, and sloshing through stagnant pools to get to the coastline, wandering on and off the overgrown trail. But on October 23rd, after a single day's hike, Muir reached the Gulf.

Today I reached the sea...yet many miles back, I caught the scent of the salt sea breeze...which conjured up Dunbar (Scotland, where he was born), and my whole childhood, that seemed to have suddenly vanished in the New World, was now restored...with one breath from the sea. I do not wonder that the weary camels coming from the scorching African deserts should be able to scent the Nile. For nineteen years my vision was bounded by forests, but to-day emerging from a multitude of tropical plants, I beheld the Gulf of Mexico stretching away unbounded, except by the sky.

Debra Lyon-Dye

How many travelers to Cedar Key have not had the same reaction after shuttling down the seemingly endless Hwy. 24 to finally emerge onto the Number Four Bridge and wide open sky?

But at this point, Muir had a dilemma: whether to set out on foot for Tampa and Key West or try to find transport in the obviously empty harbor of Cedar Keys?

To retrace his footsteps, stop at the little parkway at the east end of the No. Four bridge and imagine hiking the railroad right of way, to the left of the bridge facing town, at low tide. Then, driving into town, take a left onto Grove Street and walk the easy 1,700 foot Railroad Trestle Nature Trail, preserved by the local non-profit Florida Nature Coast Conservancy. The trail, if it continued as did the train, would come out at the Nature's Landing Condominiums, the Association of which granted the conservation easement. (At this point I must interject a local story, taken from the supposed torn out pages of Muir's journal. That while sitting on the railway bridge looking towards the current Mermaids Landing Cottages, he saw "a glistening green tail full of scales and a flash of golden hair." Thus, the name of the cottages.) Walking from the condominiums which are at the east end of Second St., towards the beach you will find several historic markers noting the importance of the site. Muir, luckily, found somewhere along the way, a little store, (probably Parsons & Hale, now the Island Hotel), "trading in quinine, alligator and rattlesnake skins," the proprietor of which, upon inquiry, told him about a cedar sawmill, one of several in town, out on Hodgson Hill which had a schooner chartered "to carry a load of lumber to Galveston, Texas." Muir decided to find the mill, wait for the ship, head to Galveston and then find transport from there.

To trace Muir's footsteps, find your way to the school house at the top of G Street and then follow the State Museum signs, but stay on Hodges until taking a left on Watson. Take a right

Cedar Key Spirit Tour

on Susan and go straight to encircle "Hodgson Hill." There Mr. Hodgson and his wife Sarah had a home and mill, although the exact location has yet to be discovered.

Muir, finding himself broke and with two weeks to wait, found Mr. Hodgson who employed him to fix the main driving pulley of his mill. Mr. Hodgson was much impressed with his mechanical skill.

He invited me to his spacious house, which occupied a hillock and commanded a fine view of the Gulf and many gems of palmy islets, called "keys" that fringe the shores like huge bouquets...Mr. Hodgson's family welcomed me with that open, unconstructed cordiality, which is characteristic of the better class of Southern people.

Shortly after arriving, Muir fell ill from malaria, now believed to have been caught during his mosquito-filled nights spent in the Bonaventure Cemetery. Trying unsuccessfully to fight the illness by swimming and ingesting lemons, he fell unconscious in a heap of saw dust at the steps of the mill lodging-house. The night watchmen assumed he was drunk and refused to assist him. "The mill hands, especially on Saturday nights, often returned from the village drunk."

He was eventually moved to the Hodgson's home where he was treated with quinine, calomel, other "milder medications," and rest. There he stayed for three months, and recorded, "I was nursed with unfailing kindness...and due to the skill and care of Mr. and Mrs. Hodgson I doubtless owe my life."

When somewhat better, as a convalescent, Muir walked the islets of Hodgson Hill making sketches and taking notes on the beauty he saw. The Historical Society Museum displays one of his sketches of Lime Key.

I...sat day after day beneath a moss-draped live oak, watching birds feeding on the shore when the tide went out. Later, I sailed in a little skiff from one key to another...the oak...growing in the dooryard of

Mr. Hodgson's house...is a grand old king, whose crown gleamed in the bright sky long ere the Spanish shipbuilders felled a single tree of this noble species...I lie here on my back for whole days beneath the ample arms of these great trees, listening to the winds and the birds... an extensive shallow...is the feeding ground of thousands of waders of all sizes, plumage, and language...it is delightful to observe the assembling of these feathered people from the woods and reedy isles.

Muir goes on to write in beautiful prose about the flora and fauna of the Cedar Keys. He describes the climate as "simply warm summer and warmer summer." Noting that the daily temperature in December is sixty-five degrees in the shade he does concede "...but on one day a little damp snow fell." In my mind's eye, I see the bundled and freezing locals passing by the flip-flop and shorts-wearing Canadian or northern tourist today.

He observes that "no portion of this coast...nor the flat border from Maryland to Texas, is quite free from malaria."

All the inhabitants of this region, whether black or white, are liable to be prostrated by the ever present fever and ague, to say nothing of the plagues of cholera and yellow fever that come and go suddenly like storms, prostrating the population and cutting gaps in it like hurricanes in the woods.

In the Cedar Keys, Muir furthers his ideas that nature is not for man to exploit and control; that the world is not man-centered; that good and bad elements of nature are but all part of the plan.

The world, we are told, was made especially for man—a presumption not supported by all the facts. A numerous class of men are painfully astonished whenever they find anything, living or dead, in all God's universe, which they cannot eat or render in some way what they call useful to themselves...sheep, for example, food and clothing "for us," whales...storehouses of oil "for us," plants...iron..."for us." But... how about those man-eating animals—lions, tigers, alligators— which smack their lips over raw man? Or...those myriads of noxious

Cedar Key Spirit Tour

insects... Doubtless man was intended for food and drink for all these? Oh, no! Not at all! ...Certain parts of the earth prove that the whole world was not made for him.

Now, it never seems to occur to these far-seeing teachers that Nature's object in making animals and plants might possibly be first of all the happiness of each one of them, not the creation of all for the happiness of one.

But...I joyfully return to the immortal truth and immortal beauty of Nature.

Having spent four months in Cedar Key, in January of 1868 Muir climbed to the Hodgson's rooftop, obviously strengthened, "...to get a view of another of the fine sunsets of this land of flowers... when "my eyes chanced to rest upon the fluttering sails of a Yankee schooner...threading the tortuous channel in the reef leading to the harbor of Cedar Key." Gathering his plants, he bade farewell to his dear friends Mr. R. W. B. Hodgson and his wife, Sarah, promising to return in twenty-five years. He remembered their kindness forever.

For twenty-five dollars he purchased passage on Captain Parson's schooner the Island Belle, bound for Cuba with a cargo of lumber. Muir sailed to Cuba, spent a month there, but finding himself again in poor health, and not finding transport to South America, longed for the "cold weather of New York." Arriving in New York in February, he stayed aboard ship until securing passage to California by way of Panama. He went on to make history, preserving Yosemite Valley, Sequoia National Park and other wilderness areas by petitioning Congress, thus earning presidential praise.

Muir did not get to South America until 44 years later in 1911, well aware of the folly of his youthful plans. He did return to Cedar Keys to find the Hodgsons, not twenty-five years later as promised, but in 1898, thirty years later. Unfortunately, Mr. Hodgson and his oldest son had both died, but he found Sarah and the rest of the family in nearby Archer. It should be noted that this was two years after the 1896 hurricane which may have caused their relocation. At first Sarah Hodgson did not recognize Muir when he surprised her in her garden, but then according to Muir, "she almost screamed, 'My California John Muir?'" Muir spent four hours reminiscing with the Hodgson family.

The eldest boy and girl remembered the stories I told them, and when they read about 'The Muir Glacier' they felt sure it must have been named for me. The way we talked over old times you may imagine.

Yes, we can imagine. John Muir is an American legend and America owes him much, but to Cedar Key and its inhabitants, John Muir owed much. The island continues to inspire with nature's healing power…offered with equal hand to the lucky occasional visitor and the long-time island resident.

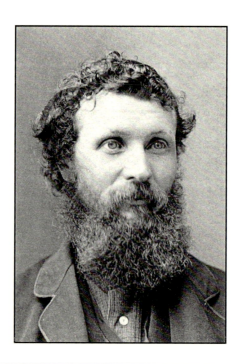

Cedar Key Spirit Tour

TOUR STOP 9
Chapter 13

Post-Civil War Boom Years

Historic Spirit Tour Stop No. Nine: Third and G Streets.

Time to move now from the bench at Third and F. Walk west down the hill, keeping the Cedar Key Bed & Breakfast to your left. This lovely 1880 structure was constructed of native yellow pine, built to house the employees of the Eagle Cedar Mill. Especially notice the large oaks which arborists date to the 1600s. Stop at the bottom of Third and face the mural of the Eagle Cedar Mill painted by Adla Kerr on one of the cottages of The Faraway Inn. The Faraway Inn was the site of the Eagle Cedar Mill from 1870 until its destruction by the 1896 hurricane.

55

Old photos reveal that the steam mill employed some 125 workers: adults, children, blacks, whites, males, and females. During the Boom Years, it, along with seventeen other mills, exported over a million cubic board feet of lumber annually from the area. Employment needs of this industry swelled the population. The details of this economy are wonderfully illustrated at the Cedar Key Historical Museum. It should be noted that after the destruction of the mill, the wood from the site was salvaged to build many of the homes in the neighborhood. The rusted iron hulk, still visible on the beach to the south of the site, is the old boiler either from the Eagle Cedar Mill or possibly the Suwannee Pine Lumber Co. which was located where the Beachfront Motel now sits.

Sometime in the forties, the Faraway Inn was built, originally named Edgewater Cottages. There was no G Street, just the beach. These lodgings have had several different owners, but at this point, it is time to tell the ghost stories of this busy and yet peaceful spot, contributed by current owners Doreen and Oliver Bauer.

The Bauers purchased the business in November of 2000. Many returning winter guests had been enjoying the cottages and gardens for years. One couple who had been coming for some ten years always stayed in Room Five. The wife told the Bauers that a man in a Civil War uniform had materialized from the cottage's television. That this, in fact, had happened several times. Also, the Paranormal Society, frequent visitors on the islands, had stayed in Cottage One and were so troubled by the "energy" coming from the old house adjacent to the cottage that they left and wouldn't go back. (This house fronts Fourth Street.) Additionally, the Bauers' cat was drawn over and over again to the Captain's Quarters, where they had an encounter of their own.

One week day, when Doreen and Oliver were replacing toilet seats in all the units, they headed to the Captain's Quarters, which was empty. Oliver started in, mumbled a quick apology, set the boxed toilet seat on a chair by the door and backed out. Doreen, close behind him, questioned who he was talking to and he said, "I thought you said the room was empty?" She affirmed that it was, there were no guests registered. Oliver stammered that he had seen an older man in there with a handle bar mustache. They knocked and slowly peeked back in but the cottage was empty. Oliver's description of the man matched exactly that of former owner, Cleve, who had died of a heart attack shortly after finishing cabinet work in Cottage One. Cleve was never seen again.

In 2014 Doreen reported that all strange occurrences had stopped. "I think the former owner was saying 'O.K. you are doing what I want you to do and I just waited to make sure you were doing the right thing. I'll stop messing with you folks.' Now even all the cats are relaxed and happy!"

I must add that this corner swirls with ghost stories told to me by many residents, but I cannot retell them all.

Note: My dilemma is that so many stories of Cedar Key ghosts have been told to me, that they in fact inhabit so many homes and buildings, that I have had to choose which to include in my account. I'm sorry for all those stories "left on the floor." Some do not fit historically, some have not been corroborated by at least three witnesses, and some are in homes where I have not contacted owners to receive permission to tell their tale.

Chapter 14

Another Seahorse Key Ghost Story

Before we leave Third Street and G, and head back up the hill towards 'town,' we will take a last glance at Seahorse Key for another story from that mysterious key. It is not the story of the "invisible dog" recently told me by visiting university students, or the story of a local author's "visitor in the middle of the night" while staying in the lighthouse, but rather a story from P. H. Day's book, *Destination Cedar Key*.

Pershing Harold Day was born east of Tallahassee, but moved to Cedar Key in 1929 at the age of eleven, and his account of strange happenings on Seahorse Key is remembered from a story he heard from Sammy Lindsey. Mr. Day retells the story of Old Man Gardner and his jilted daughter, of her suicide, and his slaying of her horse. The story concludes with the numerous accounts of the headless horse running through the sand close to shore on moonlit nights, the shadow of a headless horse.

Mr. Day writes, "A lot of mysterious things have happened around that island." He goes on to tell about a fishing trip he went on with friends Winter (Crevasse), Skinny, Charlie, and John one evening on the northwest cove of the island. Purportedly Winter, alone in his own boat, beached on the island to throw his cast net for bait. He was quite a ways from the others, but began to hear the sound of "someone slushing through the water." He knew it wasn't his fellow fisherman and decided to get in his boat and push off. He continued to hear the sound of someone or something coming through the water and so went to deeper waters. The noise continued towards him. Now alarmed, he hollered to his fishing companions, "Sammy, Skinny, John, is that you? Please let it be you!" According to P. H., he was "white as a sheet...all we could get out of him was that he wanted to go home. As far as I know that man never went fishing on that island again!"

When I told this story several years ago on a tour, a local said, "not only would Winter not fish there, but none of his family would ever fish there either." When I retold the story on Seahorse Key during a Cedar Key Lighthouse event, historian Lindon Lindsey listened to me patiently, and when I finished said, "What she says is true, but not just the Crevasse family wouldn't fish there, none of us would!"

Cedar Key Spirit Tour

TOUR STOP ⑩

Chapter 15

Boom to Bust, the 1896 Hurricane and the Ghost of a Railroad Man

Historic Spirit Tour Stop No. Ten: Read and stroll on Second Street back to town.

We need to head to town, so going back up the hill turn right on F, then left on Second Street, to make our way to the next stop. We'll walk all the way through town to Depot Street.

In 1875 Poet Sidney Lanier and British Guards Captain Frederick Townshend passed through Cedar Keys. The latter gentleman wrote in the *Bronson Artery* that the hotels were so horrific that they left them and made their way in the dark of night to stay on a south-bound steamer. "Under the guidance of a small negro boy, we again emerged into the street, and stumbling across half a mile of shaky wooden stage, often only one plank in width, pitch darkness all around, the sea beneath, at imminent risk of dunking, if not drowning, we at last reached the wharf at which lay the steamer. We soon scrambled on board her, and rousing a sleepy steward, were shown to a filthy cabin, where stifling heat, bugs, fleas, cockroaches, and mosquitoes combined to make the few remaining hours of the night anything but hours of rest. Daylight showed us the "favorite winter resort" of Cedar Keys to be a wood built village…the harbor available for vessels of not more than twelve feet of draught, and the port of call for two lines of steamers running north and south. One from New Orleans to Havana…the other a coast line touching at Cedar Keys, Manatee, and Tampa and occasionally running to Punta Rassa and Key West…advertised to run weekly, (they) are very irregular, and no dependence whatever can be placed on their days of running."

Debra Lyon-Dye

A visual image of Cedar Keys "Boom Years" is nicely captured on an 1884 *Birds Eye View Map* hanging in the Cedar Key Historical Society Museum. Lumber, oysters, turtles, fish, and sponges were harvested, ships were being built, including the 45 foot steam powered *Annie M* from Eugene Coons' boatyard on Piney Point, and the population was at its historic highpoint. Some estimated 3,000, but a more accurate figure is 2,000. Hotels were full, the railroad ran weekly, and ships steamed in and out of the harbor, past the lighthouse. Troops were passing in and out of Cedar Key, some heading south to help Cuba fight for its independence from Spain, some out west to the frontier. Warehouses of cotton, kerosene, and sponges were full; land was hard to get "even for churches," according to Fishburne; and a police force was instituted, "for the suppression of all riotous and disorderly conduct." In 1885 the "Dirt Road" was built from the mainland to the "City of Cedar Keys." Both Way Key and Atsena Otie were thriving. There were two steam mills on Atsena Otie, the largest being the world famous Eberhard Faber (Pencil) Company. The entire country was thriving as transportation and communication lines were rebuilt, the population greatly increased, and the change from agricultural to industrial economy was taking place.

However, what goes up must inevitably come down, and the tremors of the largest earthquake ever to occur in Florida, shocking the state and Cedar Key on January 12, 1879, were a portent of things to come. A second earthquake on August 31st, 1886, the Charleston Earthquake, recorded by both Light Keeper Hobday and Eliza Hearn, was part of a continuous string of disturbing events.

David Levy Yulee, now living comfortably in Washington, D. C. according to Fishburne's account, wanted to sell "his" railroad. In 1884 a deal was struck with Henry Plant, one of the kings of transportation. Plant, having an immense network of railroad, steamer, and steamship lines, was to purchase the Florida Railroad, from Fernandina to Cedar Key. However, before signing the contract, he noted that the transaction did not include the terminus of the railroad in Cedar Key, and no amount of negotiating or threatening on either side would result in the sale. Plant was furious and cursed the city: "I will wipe Cedar Key off the map. Owls will hoot in your attics and hogs will wallow in your deserted streets!" Leaving what he hoped would become a ghost town, he then made way for Tampa. The state's business and population would follow him to that city. Cedar Keyans today wonder if that curse wasn't indeed a blessing, not that it doesn't admire Tampa from some one hundred miles away.

In 1889 a madman entered Cedar Key, first hired as an Inspector of Customs, then elected to the City Council: William "Billy" Cottrell. Toni Collins, in her book *Cedar Keys Light Station,* writes of the loss of natural resources by 1890 but also of Cottrell's "reign of terror" on the now dying town. Cottrell's violence against anyone who crossed him included whippings, lashings, attempted murder, and finally murder. Businesses closed overnight as intimidated owners left by dark, never to return. Cottrell indiscriminately threatened telegraph operators, light keepers, custom inspectors, the post master, and many others. He eventually fled town with his gang of hoodlums when a Federal gunboat entered in the harbor ready to stop his violence. He finally met his end in Montgomery, Alabama, where he was shot in the face while attacking the police chief, who refused to meet him in a duel.

According to Fishburne, between Cottrell's madness, the decline in population, the exhaustion of timber and marine resources, (especially green turtle), political subdivisions, uncollected taxes, city border disputes, confusing city ordinances, and public health issues, (hogs were running the streets), over-valued property plummeted. He cites the Ice &

Cold Storage Co., falling in value from $20,000 to $4,000. By 1892 Cedar Key was a town "on the skids." An 1893 panic on the New York Stock Exchange sparked a nationwide sell-off and depression, but closer to home, the mysterious death of Piney Point Ship builder Coons, was more upsetting in the tiny island community. His widow moved to Miami.

The last blow to the already down and out community was the much written-about Hurricane of 1896, with subsequent storm surges. For the in-depth story I direct you to the excellent book, *Disaster at Dawn* by Alvin Oickle.

Records show that the late September hurricane was tight and compact, travelling just south of the Caribbean islands, swinging wide into the Gulf, therefore clearing Florida, with a surprise punch for its coastal bull's eye, Cedar Key. Then across the state to the Florida/Georgia border, on to Savannah, Washington D.C, and north all the way to lower Michigan, then Lake Ontario and Canada, all in barely 24 hours!

That fateful September, Levy County and surrounding counties were in full harvest, warehouses were full, logging camps and steam mills were working full blast, hundreds of mullet were being caught, and wild game was plentiful. A Greek sponge king was sending crews to harvest the waters around Cedar Key. The harbor was busy with traffic. A storm in the gulf was forecast to move north, bringing rain to the Carolinas. Strange tides had been noted for two days and an offshore wind was pushing water to the west. Oickle quotes James W. Beacham: "...the sea retreated to the far horizon and vast mudflats were exposed. The people on islands up and down the coast simply had to stay put and wait for whatever was coming." Little did they know what was coming!

The morning of the 29th, a forecaster in Atlanta finally predicted the storm that the islands of Cedar Keys were already experiencing, as "screaming winds" and a ten foot "wall of surging water" crashed upon them. Hitting the island of Atsena Otie first, ten year old Velma Crevasse screamed to her family, "Look at the water coming!" As house after house was swept away, only a few citizens of Cedar Key saw the ten foot surge coming their way next. Second St. was quickly under eight feet of water, coquina foundations crumbling. Cooking stoves, lit for morning, if not in the deep water, were blown over and fires swept from building to building. On the outer islands, along the Suwannee River, and in normally protective bayous, poor souls clung to palm trees, boats, and finally debris. There was little mercy.

Cedar Key and Atsena Otie suffered massive damage: The Town Improvement Co. building and most of the homes it owned were lost, the two story Bettelini Hotel and Schlemmer House were two of the many buildings burned, the large sailing vessel "Luna Davis" lay marooned in the city center where it remained for many weeks. Buildings along Second St., if not destroyed by the storm surge or fire or winds, were wrecked from debris as the water receded. The ice factory, warehouses along the wharf, city sidewalks, most of the churches, and almost every steam mill were a total loss. Water craft of every shape and size, timber, farms, oyster beds, transportation and commerce: gone in a matter of hours. Additionally, four miles of railroad track had to be totally rebuilt.

Miraculously, Way Key suffered no loss of life. According to the *Florida Daily Citizen:*

The islands that were damaged most, and on which nearly all of the loss of life occurred, were Shell Mound, Deer Island, Cat Island, Rattlesnake Island, Axe Island, Black Point Island, Bettelini Island, Lone Cabbage Island, Scale Island, Kiss-Me-Quick Island, and numerous other smaller islands. Nearly all of those who were saved clung to saplings. They did not go near the trees with large trunks as they were invariably blown to the ground by the wind. The flexible cabbage palmetto was able to withstand the fury of the wind...

Oickle has documented at least 31 deaths on the islands off Way Key, or Cedar Key proper, including four "spongers." However, the "Florida Daily Citizen" on October 3rd wrote, "the fate of many of the spongers off Cedar Key will never be known and they will be reported as 'missing and not accounted for." Estimates run from seven to eight hundred, but this figure is the subject to much debate. The national death toll stands at 130. These figures, of course, do not account for the many deaths that occurred after the storm due to injuries, accidents, snake bite, or subsequent lack of medical care.

According to Ellen Tooke, who moved to Atsena Otie after the hurricane, as many as 35 families continued to live on the island. She documented her "sun-filled days" on the island in an interview by the publication *Search for Yesterday*.

The mills that were not totally destroyed on the Cedar Keys milled the wood that lay waste from the storm. But, within a year or two, all of the once thriving mills, including Atsena Otie's major employer, Eberhard Faber, would fall silent.

Cedar Key's population was 700 in 1900 and has only grown by a few hundred in the last 120 years, thus somewhat preserved in time.

In 1910 Cedar Key had one hotel. The last family had left Atsena Otie, many small buildings having been floated over to Way Key or Cedar Key proper to be reused. One of those was a mill house which became the home/office of the Standard Manufacturing Company, a producer of palm fiber brooms. (This site is the current location of the condominiums Old Fenimore Mill and previous location of a saw mill.) Founded by Dr. Dan Andrews, after learning the process from and hiring St. Clair Whitman, the enterprise was a Godsend to the community, employing some 100 Cedar Key residents at a time until 1952. (It was forced to close for several years after World War II, due to lack of workers.) Dr. Andrews built a second story and porches on the old mill house and lived there with his wife and two sons. The building was later donated by the family to the Cedar Key Historical Museum and in 1995 moved to D Street, behind the main building. It houses an exhibit of the process of turning palm fiber to brooms. Further information is now available in a book by Dr. John Andrews, "Cedar Key Fiber and Brush Factory." (The St. Clair Whitman house is located at the State Museum on SW 166th Court.)

In 1915 the Cedar Keys Light Station was too remote to be converted to electric. Fewer and fewer vessels required its light of safety, and so it was declared surplus and services discontinued. Light keeper Gardner and his wife stayed on Seahorse Key.

In the 1920s electricity finally reached the island community, and by the 1930's telephone service was offered to residents.

Train service continued to Cedar Key, both freight and passenger, until 1932, when it became too unprofitable. But one caboose conductor was seen well after the last train ran. So I conclude this chapter with another "story."

The office of Nature Coast Landing is actually a portion of the original depot station of the railroad. The line ran parallel to what is now Highway 24 on a series of low islands, still visible to the south while driving on the only road into town. It went past the station to Dock Street to unload and load cargo, then backed onto a track on the current beach, to then be able to run back to Fernandina. The cute names of the neighborhoods it passed through were derived from the railroad days: Hug Me Tight, Kiss Me Quick.

Ghost of a Railroad Man:

One of the first "ghost stories" I was told in Cedar Key was about the red light seen from Highway 24, along the path of the old railroad bed. Supposedly, there was a man whose work was to swing the red lantern from the back door of the caboose to signal an "all clear." This same gentlemen did it for many years. He died about the time the train finished its last trip into Cedar Key. No one remembers how he died, but for years a red light continued to be seen by local residents swinging back and forth over the deserted tracks, signaling the "all clear."

Cedar Key Spirit Tour

TOUR STOP 11

Chapter 16

Miss Susie, the Midwife of Cedar Key

Historic Spirit Tour Stop No. Eleven: Vacant Lot just east of the Island Hotel, now a community garden.

After leaving Depot Street we head back toward the Island Hotel, pausing at a lot which once contained the home of one very busy lady.

In the first half of the twentieth century, women in Cedar Key, more often than not, called "Miss Susie and be quick about it," when it came time to birth a child. Mother of twelve children, Susie Coburn Bishop brought many Cedar Key children safely into the world, including several of her own grandchildren.

Born in Carrabelle, Florida in 1875, Miss Susie, the "Midwife of Cedar Key," walked to the homes of her patients carrying a small case containing supplies that she made herself. Her case, midwife kit, and a bundle of her papers were donated to the Cedar Key Historical Society Museum by her family and are on display there. The display includes a pattern with instructions for making the nurse's hygienic nose and mouth covers out of heavy muslin, sugar sacks, or flour sacks, using tape ties. She had no assistant and payment in those days was naturally meager.

Her services were needed long before training was available, other than her own experience; but she was officially certified by the State Board of Health. An official document from Jacksonville reads, "Certificate of Registry Granted to Mrs. William Bishop, Midwife, Cedar Keys, Florida, who has met the requirements of Chapter 14760, Law of 1931. Certificate expires December 31, 1933."

In August of 1934 she attended a Program of The West Florida Institute for Midwives at Florida A & M College in Tallahassee. The program reads:

Sunday-Sermon and Music.

Monday-Classes and Health Examinations, Lecture on Syphilis in Pregnancy.

Tuesday-Morning Devotions, Lectures on Prenatal Care and Responsibilities of the Midwife to her patient. Evening-Moving Picture Show, Auditorium.

Wednesday-Devotions, Lecture on Rural Sanitation. Evening-Play, Dance of the Bones.

Thursday-Devotions, Lectures on Tuberculosis in Pregnancy, Postnatal Care, and Care of the Teeth. Evening-Guest of College President, 8 p.m.

Friday-Devotions, Lectures on Accidents, Complications, and Immunizations. Farewell songs by Midwives.

Midwife Bishops' paperwork from that training included a final checklist of sorts:

--*Model Bag Demonstration*

--*Inspection of Bags*

--*Making Cord Dressings*

--*Making Wipes*

--*Folding and wrapping Supplies*

Midwives were instructed to complete and mail monthly reports the first of every month "neatly and correctly." Failure to do so could result in loss of certification. Those reports included the number of cases "engaged for," the number delivered, the number of times the physician was called, number of live births, and number of still births. The Midwife also had questions to answer; "Did you put the drops of SILVER NITRATE in the eyes of all babies born where you attended the mother this month? Did you have any cases of sore eyes in the newborns this month? What did you do?" It is interesting that the weight and length of the baby was not required information.

For each birth a Bureau of Child Hygiene Board of Health Certificate was completed. Two books containing certificates were found in Midwife Bishop's professional items at the museum. The certificates recorded: Child's Name, Address and the Date of Birth, Mother's Name and Age, Father's Name and Age, Parents' Color, Schooling, and Marital Status, Date of Expected Confinement, Attendant, Number of Living Children, Number of Children Total, and Person referring Midwife to Family. A "Period of Confinement" in those days meant the number of days after birth that the mother was confined to bed to decrease blood loss and for the purposes of healing.

The first of two books found began with the May 7, 1935, birth of James Emmitt Purvis and ended on March 4, 1938, with the birth of Charles Austin Baird. In that period of time there were 14 births recorded, all "live" and all "white." The second book began January 19, 1939, with the birth of James Gerald Wilkerson and ended with the birth of Carolyn Rebecca Osteen on April 15, 1940. In that period of time Midwife Bishop attended six births, all "live", five "white", and one "colored." Unfortunately, the following year, her life of hard work and service was over.

Laura Jean Bishop Delaino, Miss Susie's granddaughter, recalls that "Big Mama," as she was affectionately known by her large family, died in 1941 of a heart attack at the age of 66. In a 2015 interview, Mrs. Delaino, now 84, noted, "I was eleven when she died, but I remember she was always working, somehow also involved with a community sewing project, those were the WPA days. I think the sewing room was in the old McNulty building where the dentist is now. I remember she was a great seamstress and I inherited that little gift from her. I remember she made a beautiful pinafore for me. But back in those days you didn't even hear the word pregnant until you were much older." (The McNulty house is noted as Bodiford's Drug Store in the Museum's Walking Tour Guide Book.)

"Big Mama" or "Miss Susie" lived on 2nd Street two doors down from the Island Hotel in a two story house that is now a vacant lot. Later she lived in "Kiss Me Quick" in the clapboard house at the corners of Live Oak and Grove Streets, restored by the same couple who by a quirk of fate also purchased the site of her former home on 2nd St. The photos provided by Mrs. Delaino show Miss Susie sitting on the porch of that house during a large family gathering, just before her death. She is all smiles in the photos as she hugs children and grandchildren, in-laws and "out-laws." A rather grim picture of

Cedar Key Spirit Tour

her is located in the Historical Society Museum in the Andrews Building, along with the doctors of Cedar Key.

When asked about the doctor at the time of Miss Susie's career as a midwife, Mrs. Delaino says that it was Dr. James Turner. She remembers a family story: her grandmother liked to brag that when women asked Dr. Turner questions about pregnancy or delivering or caring for little babies, he used to say, "You ask Miss Susie, she's had more children than I have!"

A note was found amongst Miss Susie's things which reminds us of the perils of the past and her hope in the future. In her hand she wrote: "Today we seldom hear of the diseases which a few centuries ago brought illness and death to thousands of people every year. A person could consider himself lucky if he reached old age without suffering from bubonic plague, small pox, typhoid, cholera, dysentery, diphtheria, tuberculosis, or malaria."

"Miss Susie" was considered a Godsend in the little community of Cedar Key and many literally owe their lives to her and her good work. She is buried in the Cedar Key City Cemetery alongside her husband, "Big Papa," in the Bishop Coburn family plot.

Debra Lyon-Dye

TOUR STOP ⑫

Chapter 17

Miss Bessie

Historic Spirit Tour Stop No. Twelve: The Island Hotel on Second Street, (cross the street to face it).

When Bessie Fitzgerald Gibbs and her husband, Loyal C. Gibbs, both fresh from New York City, rode into Cedar Key in a Ford station wagon in 1946, their lives and that of the tiny town's forever changed. But my research to chronicle their story begins with a bit of a mystery, an almost 30-year-old mystery.

Long fascinated by the legend of Miss Bessie and the influence of an "outsider" who became an insider in the isolated fishing village of Cedar Key, I have been curious about the fresh decorations which have been lovingly placed on her grave since the 1980s. For years I have politely asked, "Are you the person who tends Miss Bessie's grave at the Cedar Key Cemetery?" To which I have received at least fifty polite "No, but ask so and so…" While her ashes were spread in the Gulf near her husband's, her grave marker sits to the left of the entrance of the cemetery on Gulf Boulevard. Someone has been lovingly tending the grave and I'd like to know WHOM? After years of trying to discover the origin of the silk flowers and whatnots that appear every three months or so, someone even joked, "Maybe it's Gibby, sneaking in from the Gulf!" Perhaps.

Bessie Fitzgerald Gibbs, born April 7, 1911, was one of twelve children of a Columbus, Georgia school teacher, according to the vertical files at the Cedar Key Historical Society Museum. Her mother sent her north to further her education. Bessie attended Boston University; Columbia University in New York, albeit briefly; The Fanny Farmer School of Cookery, and a secretarial school. An undated newspaper article at the museum by Jack McClintoch states, "She worked in kitchens and chorus lines but graduated with a degree in Home Economics."

Whitey McMullen reported on March 2, 1958, "Loyal C. Gibbs, a native of New York with a degree in Hotel Management from Cornell University, met Bessie in Daytona Beach in 1928…. they married in 1929."

Loyal C. Gibbs, nicknamed "Gibby," worked for The New York Life Insurance Co. as a hotel advisor and according to notes obtained from Bessie's sister, Melba Franklin, by the museum, "Bessie and her husband got real tired of the New York rat race and came south." They looked around until they found Cedar Key. It was said that the (Island) hotel was a whorehouse at the time. C. J. Fitzgerald, our brother from Minnesota, came down and helped her build the bar and get the business started."

Records show that Gibby and a Cornell classmate bought the hotel in 1946 as equal business partners from Miss Hatie Feinburg of Atlantic City. It is well documented on the Island Hotel website that Bessie was not particularly impressed with the hotel. The first night she stayed there, she slept in an upright chair not wanting to catch anything. The first thing she did was clean the building from stem to stern. Some say the hotel was Gibby's idea, but that Bessie's drive developed it.

Dudley Clendinen of the St. Petersburg Times, wrote, "They... had come to a lapsed city on a remote island, a quietly expiring fishing village named Cedar Key, whose cedars had all been cut up into pencils the century before and whose population had vanished with the cedars."

Indeed, at that time, the town's population was less than 800, as World War II had taken its toll on the town. The Standard Manufacturing Co., which made palm fiber brooms, was forced to close during the war due to "lack of workers." Nearly a quarter of the town's residents had left to serve in the military and many did not return, finding employment elsewhere. (Note: The factory was able to reopen in 1950.)

In Historical Society notes, former Cedar Key Commissioner J. Quitman Hodges, who was born in the hotel, reminisced, "Bessie bought the hotel the same time I bought the house next door to the hotel. She had birds and monkeys and everything else."

Again quoting her sister Melba, "There was an old Western Union Telegraph in the lobby, so Bessie knew everything that was going on in Cedar Key. Bessie kept lovebirds and canaries in the yard."

In Bessie's own words, "We started out featuring a plate of 'all the fish you can eat for $1.' The price had to go up, of course." Bessie's goal was to make the hotel into a state, if not a national destination. In Historical Society notes, Sandy Gravely remembered, "Focusing on the comfort of the guests was Bessie's goal and the staff's forte. They offered reasonable rates and seasonal affordable food."

It would probably surprise some readers that the Gibbs actually tried to modernize the hotel, shocking some with a television in the lobby, adding air conditioning to some of the rooms, and furnishing the rooms in sleek, modern furniture with simple lines.

An early hotel advertisement offered rooms from $5 daily for a single without a bath to $84 weekly for a double room with private bath. Eventually they had 25 rooms and a basement apartment to let. The atmosphere was island casual and when one guest inquired about a safe, Bessie is quoted as saying, "If you have anything that valuable, bring it down here. I'll put it in my safe. I'm not running any damn Holiday Inn!"

In the hot off-season of the summer of 1948, an artist perpetually down on her luck showed up at the hotel with her daughter. Helen Tooker, daughter in tow, agreed to dress up the drab hotel in exchange for room and board. An arrangement agreeable to both Bessie and the artist was made, as funds were low for both.

Tooker's daughter's memoir, *Skunk Stew,* describes those Cedar Key days. An accomplished author and artist, Helen Parramore, Ph.D., recalls:

We got into our truck and bumbled around from one Florida town to another until we came to Cedar Key, a small, isolated fishing village on the Gulf of Mexico. We spent the summer there redecorating the bar. In 1948, the town had no doctor, no police, no fire department, no movie theater, and a very small one-room library. The thousand or so residents had lived there marrying each other or those from neighboring towns ever since their forefathers wrested the area from the Indians.

Debra Lyon-Dye

The hotel at the end of Main Street put up sportsmen who came to the town from Georgia, Alabama, and north Florida to do serious fishing, and the hotel bar was the watering hole for visiting fishermen as well as an assortment of local residents.

My mother and I spent our first summer in Florida there, stretching one job into another—painting sepia murals of Cedar Key scenes in the spacious, open upstairs hall, decorating table tops in the dining room, converting a storage area into a bar with murals lining the room to create the illusion of space in what had been a large closet, and putting old Neptune, with two naked mermaids on his lap, smack over the bar.

Helen Tooker, with her reluctant daughter's assistance, also illustrated a large wall hanging showing the Cedar Key islands and Miss Bessie's hotel flyers and menus. An early decorated menu entices visitors with, "See the murals of Local Scenes in our own Cocktail Bar--Beer-Wine-Mixed Drinks-Cordials." Thus freshened, the hotel's artistic ambiance now matched the artistry that was created in the kitchen by Miss Bessie and her black cook Catherine Johnson. A native Cedar Keyan adds, "Big Buster" as Catherine was called, lived up on "the hill" on 6th Street with her husband, Hatchet Johnson.

Bessie set high standards for her dining room, only using fresh seafood and seasonal vegetables bought from local vegetable peddlers. Portions were hearty. An original brochure reads, "Our food is cooked to order and comes to you fresh daily from the waters surrounding Cedar Key." Good food took time and she was quoted as saying, "I just can't prepare food for people who are in a hurry."

"Back in those days you put your order in at the front counter and waited," recalls Henry Coulter. "I brought the tickets back to the kitchen. Then you were called in when your food was ready. I worked three or four nights a week with my grandmother, Maggie Coulter, when I was 12 or 13. People used to line up out the door." In a 2015 interview, native Cedar Keyan Henry Lee

Coulter, nephew of Clyde Coulter who drove the Greyhound bus line from Cedar Key to Jacksonville and grandson of Clyde David Coulter, Sr., a train conductor for the Cedar Key to Fernandina Seaboard Airline Railroad, remembers those days well. He stayed overnight in many rooms, even in Miss Bessie's, Number 29. He also carried luggage for a "quarter or two quarter tip." He continued, "On a good night we served a hundred dinners. A typical dinner was whatever fish was in season, either broiled or fried, and hush puppies. Green turtle steaks were also on the menu. Every now and again, I mean **every** now and again, I got to eat shrimp. They didn't have any hamburgers then, but my Aunt Verona used to make the Key Lime Pies."

An old menu found at the museum offers "Dinners in Season:"

Stone Crab…$3.50   Crab Cakes…$2.25   Crab Fingers…$2.25 Trout…$2   Deviled Crab…2.75   Crab au Gratin…$2.75   Soft Shell Crab…$3.00   Green Turtle Steaks…$3.00   Shrimp…$2.00 Pompano…$4.00   Scallops…$2.00   Lisa (Mullet)…$1.50   Fried Oysters…$2.50   Mariner's Platter…$2.50   Broiled Lobster Tails…$3.50   One-half Southern Fried Chicken…$2.00   Baked Ham…$2.00   Seafood Cocktail…$.75

Famous Island Hotel Turtle Chowder, Heart of Palm (Swamp Cabbage) Salad, and Hush Puppies served with all meals. Vegetables, Salad, Dessert and Drink included in the price of all meals.

Hotel specialties: Seafood Bisque, Turtle Chowder, Lime Pie, Orange Custard Cake, and Poached Fish with White Wine (when in the mood to cook it).

Dining Room Lunch 12-2. Dinner 5-9. Sunday Noon until 8.

Miss Bessie was known for her well-seasoned temper, salty vocabulary, and sense of humor. She was known to chastise customers if necessary, and woe be to the customer who left vegetables on his plate. One of her more printable quips was, "After I worked so hard to cook you a nice dinner I expect you to eat it. NOW EAT THOSE VEGETABLES!"

In 1950 a hurricane hit Cedar Key, sixteen hours of hell according to those who lived it, a small but intense storm that came back and hit twice. "Easy," as it was later called by "people far away" took roofs and homes and businesses. Gibby and seven guests rode out the hurricane in the hotel, but most of the town's residents eventually rode out the storm "up at the brick school house" in what is now the Elementary School. The hurricane took the hotel roof and filled the upstairs with several feet of water. It is documented that it rained over 24 inches. The water ran down the downstairs walls, damaging old King Neptune and his mermaids. Miss Bessie's collection of birds which she kept in the yard, according to her sister, also disappeared in the storm.

Gibby's partner was anxious to get out after that and sold his half to Gibby and Bessie. For the hurricane damage, Gibby "...got half value when he got $12,000 insurance for water damage." The Gibbs spent extra money, according to Bessie, when later running for office, to rebuild the roof in a historic manner.

Repair and rebuild they did, working together...loving Cedar Key as they went along, Cedar Key loving them right back. Soon the hotel became "the destination" that Bessie and her loyal Gibby worked for. Bessie's dining room and Gibby's *Neptune Lounge* soon welcomed many rich and famous. Over the 27 years that they operated the hotel, guests included Governor Claude Kirk and other Florida governors; authors Pearl Buck, Marjorie Kinnan Rawlings, and Harry Reed; singers Vaughn Monroe, Mell Tillis, and Tennessee Ernie Ford; and actors Francis Langford, Myrna Loy, Leif Ericson, Mell Tillis, and Richard Boone.

In the 1950s the town park was dedicated and a series of Beauty Contests were held to "bring in the tourists." People work real hard after a hurricane to rebuild their reputation as a place to come visit and spend money. Fall festivals became the time to showcase the best seasonal seafood. A 1957 newspaper photo in the museum shows 13 stunning Beauty Contest contestants standing in front of Sally Tileston's storefront which reads, *Artists of Cedar Key Gallery,* Visitors Welcome.

Bessie and Big Buster's food gained national recognition, written up in numerous magazines including *National Geographic, The New York Times, Gourmet Magazine* and many others. The *Applied Photography Magazine* published by Eastman Kodak gushed about her Fish Chowder, "Fish of the day married to the freshest of vegetables of the season in an essence of fish stock through which strays the elusive elegance of a magical herbal blend." The article was complete with a photo shoot of Cedar Key.

However, the Island Hotel, Bessie and "Big Buster" will forever be known for creating their signature *Island Hotel Heart of Palm Salad.* Again according to Eastman Kodak's publication, "Chopped hearts of tender young palms tossed with crisp lettuce and an unbelievably exotic dressing reminiscent of peanuts and ice cream." Here copied from an original hotel receipt is the recipe.

Heart of Palm Salad:

Slivered lettuce, slivered palm hearts, pineapple chunks, chopped dates, chopped crystalized ginger. Add palm dressing: 3 cups mayonnaise, 1 cup vanilla ice cream, 4 tbsp. peanut butter, 2 drops green food coloring.

Make it easy on yourself and go to the Island Hotel where it is still on the menu!

In 1958 the Gibbs gave the hotel a facelift adding the second floor veranda, lining the upstairs porch with rocking chairs, "in keeping with JFK's (John Fitzgerald Kennedy) love of rocking chairs"

1961 was a year of personal crisis for Miss Bessie. Her beloved husband of 33 years died. Her Gibby was gone. Gibby, bar tender, bouncer, and loyal husband of the boss. He once remarked, "Where else could you run a resort hotel wearing a sports shirt and shorts?" His body was cremated and ashes returned to Cedar Key for a burial at sea. Due to bad weather and uncooperative tides, his last boat trip was postponed and Bessie placed his remains on the counter behind the bar. When questioned about the appropriateness of this, Bessie sharply responded, "Why not? That's where he was happiest!" Gibby was finally laid to rest out at Channel Marker 32 by his wife and friends. Bessie commented later that just such a burial was what she wanted when the time came. According to friends, "She never had another fella."

October of the following year, the world held its breath as the Soviet Union and United States came very close to nuclear war. A disagreement over missile placement and a U. S.-led landing in Cuba had escalated to a fever pitch. At Cuba's request, the Soviet Union had installed nuclear warheads in Cuba, 60 miles from Key West. Television sets all over America advised citizens to get ready, and students were drilled, "Get under your desk, duck and cover!" A young Henry Coulter remembers that he and most of the other boys in high school were happy to help sandbag the walls of the basement under the hotel. In retrospect he wonders, "Don't know what would have happened since we didn't reinforce the ceiling." In hindsight we all now know there is no preparing for a nuclear war. But "everyone loved Miss Bessie and was happy to help."

With the love and help of a family of friends, Bessie continued to run the hotel. "Everybody loved Miss Bessie, she just had that kind of personality. She had a real big heart and never had much money because she gave it away." Comments like these by Henry Coulter are echoed from townspeople who knew her. "She was our most precious asset." "Bessie didn't have any enemies, everybody liked her." "Bessie would bail somebody out of jail if she thought they needed to be." "Bessie filled her (Edsel) station wagon with food and brought it to whatever house needed it." "She sure could take a joke." "She didn't put up with any guff and once told a filthy drunk to go home and take a bath, promptly handing him a bar of soap!"

Bessie's first interest in civic affairs happened when the Hindalls came to town and bought the "chicken coup" at 4th and G Streets. Their plan was to tear the structure down and erect a new house. But Bessie and others knew the building was the oldest residence in Cedar Key and fought to keep it from being destroyed. Her sisters said, "She raised Cain!" They luckily succeeded and today the pre-Civil War "Block House" as it is now referred, still stands gazing out to the Gulf. She worked for fourteen years to create a museum for St. Clair Whitman's seashell and artifact collection, which is now a State Museum on S. W. 166th Court.

"Bessie was not afraid to make herself heard," according to Bertie Mae Richburg's comments in Historical Society notes, "She called President Eisenhower and talked to him on the phone. She also talked to the governor and president of the University of Florida. Bessie was a legend. "If you ever knew Bessie, you would never forget her…there will never be another Bessie."

Bessie's efforts helped put Cedar Key on the map. Notes found quote Sandy Gravely: "The hotel served as a tourist information center and an unofficial Chamber of Commerce." Bessie also set an example of how to deal with state officials. Judge Jimmy Adkins wrote in his recollections, "When the state inspector and tax man came, Bessie's first reaction was to sell the hotel. We thought about it together and decided to secede. The only tax and all regulations would be set by Bessie."

Bessie was also responsible for fireworks in Cedar Key, once shooting them from the hotel balcony, arousing the attention of local officials to which she responded, "I don't care if it is against the law shooting them off inside the city!" Later on the Fourth of July she and a group set off fireworks at Piney Point, actually setting Ginnie Dickey on fire with a Roman candle.

Her escapades were well known in Cedar Key including one boat trip clear to Galveston, Texas, according to the notes of former commissioner, neighbor, and friend J. Quitman Hodges. He especially remembered her monkey who was addicted to Manhattans because when he entered the bar, people would buy him one. Bessie had to use Manhattans to get him down from Virginia Dickey's palm tree on one occasion. "Bessie found out that something that lives in a tree and pees cannot be housebroken."

A colorful character to be sure, Bessie went on to be City Commissioner, Judge, Fire Chief, Member of the Planning Board and Mayor. Her first entrance into elected office was out of concern for the appearance of Cedar Key. "I wanted to get on the city council to form a zoning board to limit the tiny trailers marring our old fishing village, and to get some of the rusting hulks of automobiles out of sloppy people's yards."

A May 26, 1975, St. Pete' Times article reads, "Bessie went crabbing on the sand bars in diamond earrings, and in between the good times, she started the Cedar Key Sidewalk Art Festival." After a series of seafood festivals, usually in the fall, springtime street dances, art shows, bathing suit and beauty contests and events sponsored by the Suwannee River Valley Association, the exact day for the beginning of the festival is not easily pinned down. Locals actually involved in the beginning differ, I believe, due to the different events. I have been quoted '63, '64, '65, and '69 and do not want to call one right and one wrong. Promoters recently celebrated its 50th year in 2014, making the date 1964.

Cedar Key Spirit Tour

Miss Thelma (McCain) told me that Miss Bessie presented the idea to the city and told them that the day the festival cost the city any money, that they would "discontinue it...and it never did!" Everyone agrees Miss Bessie, Bertie Mae Richburg and Sally Tileston started the festival; most agree the idea was hatched in the bar. Bessie once remarked, "I modeled it after the Greenwich Village art festival I remembered from years ago." In 2005 the festival was renamed the Old Florida Celebration of the Arts and with a cadre of volunteers, the tradition flourishes. Though taxing on a town of 800 when 10, 20, even 30,000 visitors engulf it, the artists, visitors, school, businesses and community all benefit.

Bessie, in the 1960s, busy with the running of a town and sole proprietor of the hotel, could still be found behind the bar, drinking beer from a can, clad in shorts or a Mumu, donning dangly earrings. The once 114-pound former chorus girl was a serious clothes horse with a fashionista's collection upstairs to be shared with anyone with similar interests. "I love clothes and anybody who loves 'em." She also created some unforgettable blender drinks including "Mullets Blood," rum, daiquiri mix, and ice...swirled with a hand full of cherries for the blood. It was the 'good ole' days.' Late at night she could often be seen sitting in the porch swing of her second floor veranda, looking down 2nd Street.

By 1970, Bessie was only 59 but already suffering from arthritis. Soon she endured two back operations, the second one leaving her in a wheelchair. She had to be carried up and down the steps of the hotel. Finally, she suffered an inflammation of the lining of her spinal column. She thought about selling and retiring. In a newspaper interview, preserved in the museum's vertical file, she spoke about her retirement and life beyond that.

I would still like to see modern cabins at the hotel and a swimming pool. But when I sell, I want to write a cookbook and a book about what women should know and a book about Cedar Key, this town is steeped in history...maybe buy a cottage but stay in Cedar Key. I love this place. I'd like to see an excursion boat up the Suwannee River... and around the islands...and adopt the council manager form of government and see Cedar Key's Main Street restored to old Florida style.

Bessie did sell the Island Hotel in 1973 and buy a little wooden cottage on Hwy. 24 a few doors west of the Blue Desert Restaurant, where there is now a vacant lot. Friends, including Fire Chief George Daniels, helped her get up when she fell, took her around town in a gas-powered golf cart, and brought her favorite foods. But Bessie never had time to write her books. Just two years after selling the hotel, in the middle of a May night, she made two calls, one to the Fire Department and one to Chief Daniels, screaming that her house was on fire. Hearing her cries, neighbors and Chief Daniels who, living just down the street, arrived in less than five minutes. They could do nothing to save her. The little wooden cottage was completely engulfed in fire. Bessie perished alone on the floor. This time none of her beloved friends could help her. The cause of the fire was investigated but never determined.

Bessie's remains were cremated, and laid to rest as near to Gibby's at Channel Marker 32 as her sister, Melba Franklin, Episcopal priest Father Wells Folsom, and 12 other friends could do, on a last boat ride on Henry Brown's crab boat. Henry Coulter's uncle, Clyde, spread her ashes and Melba set a heart-shaped wreath of ferns and orchids into the water. Dudley Clendinen, St. Pete' Times reporter and friend was invited to go along on Bessie's last boat ride. "In a sweating sun...out on a boat with family and friends, whisky for company, and a priest to see her properly down, Bessie got what she wanted."

An era was over. Memorial funds, at Bessie's request, went to the Episcopal Church, of which she was a member, to fund a new church organ. Cedar Key's "most precious asset" was gone.

With a town full of people who loved and remembered her dearly, it would probably be impossible to find out who was still tending her grave some 30 years later. For a while, I assumed it was her nieces and nephews who occasionally visited, but then determined that it was not. So, finally, I left a note in a waterproof baggie on Bessie's grave marker, politely asking the identity of the person and leaving my phone number. In a final tribute to a legend, a grateful citizen who never even knew Bessie called me and admitted to her good deed, a good deed quietly done for 30 years. Since 1985, Pat Deverin felt an obligation to honor a great woman to whom the town owed much, by keeping up her grave marker. In a fitting spirit of goodness and community, a mystery is solved.

Chapter 18

The Ghosts of the Island Hotel

While the Island Hotel on Second Street is famous for its fine food, comfortable lodging, and warm hospitality, it is also very well known for its paranormal activity. The hotel's thirteen documented ghosts are described on its website, IslandHotel-CedarKey.com. Paranormal societies frequently visit the hotel and numerous YouTube videos reveal their findings; search Island Hotel, Cedar Key ghosts. In 1999, Fox Network even filmed a segment at the hotel for its "Haunted Inns and Mansions" series.

The portal for the thirteen ghosts is believed to be Room 29, the former room of deceased owner Bessie Gibbs. Bessie is also the most dominant spirit, but as was her style, she accommodates:

A small black boy who worked for the hotel running errands during the Civil War. He was believed to have been about nine years old. If you are in the Neptune Bar, envision a set of stairs that ran down to the basement at the end of the bar, under the tiny lounge. The stairs have since been walled up, but I have seen the stairs from the basement with friends and former owners, Tony and Dawn. The story goes that the child was believed to have stolen from the hotel and chased down the stairs by the owner or manager. He disappeared, but many years later was discovered by workmen charged with cleaning out the building's cistern, presumably drowned. It is said that he still "peeks about," and he may be the source of the "wet floor stories," which I will enumerate later.

A Confederate soldier, in full uniform, very frequently seen at daybreak, upstairs, saluting the morning sky. While he makes frequent appearances, they are very brief, as he dissolves into thin air. He has also been known to stand at the top of the stairs looking down. During the Civil War, the building was occupied by the Union Army and therefore one of the few buildings in town not burned down. Towards the end of the war, once Cedar Key was "retaken," it housed the officers of the south. No one knows any details about this poor soul.

A small-waisted lady in black, often seen downstairs by the hotel staff. According to Molly, friend and employee at the hotel for many years under many owners, the lady is 40ish, frequently holding a water pitcher, wearing a long black dress, and having hair pinned up under a modest little black hat. Molly says, "I look up and someone is standing there; when I glance back she is gone." This same vision has been seen and repeated by many others. The local story is that about the turn of the century there was a woman in black who ate in the hotel dining room. On her way home she perished when her carriage turned over. This lady in black carrying the water pitcher may also be responsible for the "wet floor stories."

Simon Feinberg, second owner of Parsons & Hale's General Store, as the Island Hotel was originally known, converting it to The Bay Hotel in 1915. He leased the hotel to a Mr. W. L. Markham and went home to Tallahassee. He was forced to return, however, in May of 1919, as Mr. Markham had stopped paying him all he was due. He was further enraged upon arrival at the discovery of a copper still secreted above the roof in the Annex Building, and evidence of a bar, this being the beginning of the Prohibition Years. When Feinberg confronted the manager he was calmed down and placated with a huge dinner from the hotel's kitchen and told that all would be well, all moneys due paid very shortly, and the still and subsequent bar shut down. He then went to bed in Room 33 and fell into a deep sleep. A sleep, however, from which he was never to awaken. As Tom, a previous owner said, "It is pretty much common knowledge that what his family alleged was correct, that he was poisoned." Simon Feinberg, a short balding man, with grey sideburns, is known as the "Wandering Ghost" at the hotel and appears briefly at night, sometimes upstairs but more often than not near the downstairs kitchen pantry. The hotel's website says that, "He…is harmless at least if your name isn't Markham."

A friendly or shy ghost who divides her time between Rooms 27 and 28 and is reputed to be a murdered prostitute from Prohibition Days, when according to the hotel's website it was a "speakeasy and brothel." She is dressed in white, floats through the walls, kisses sleeping guests gently on the cheek and then disappears. She likes to sit on beds, leaving the tiny indentation of her bum. Molly once told me an amusing story about two elderly sisters who checked into one of the rooms. They unpacked, came downstairs, had dinner in the dining room, and went into the bar to have a "hot toddy." One of the sisters went upstairs to use their room's bathroom, only to return irate, complaining that someone was in their room. Since Molly had double duty as desk clerk and bartender, she apologized and checked her log. No, no one else had reserved that room. She went up with the two sisters and found no one, but the well-made bed revealed the tiny impression of someone sitting ever so lightly there. Molly apologized again, the sisters spent the night, and the shy ghost did not make another appearance that night. She has also been seen in the waitress station, very early in the evening.

Other ghosts, according to a séance held at the hotel: including two very tall Native Americans believed buried in the courtyard; a fisherman; an unidentified tall, thin man; three others about which little is known; and of course, Bessie Gibbs.

Bessie Gibbs, the "most dominant spirit," owned the hotel from

1946 to 1973 and lived there all of those years. After she sold the hotel she moved to a cottage on Hwy. 24 and perished in a house fire. A victim of a spinal disease, she was wheel chair bound and unable to get out of the terrible flames. Locals tell me there was nothing suspicious about the fire, but it was investigated. Janice Coupe, in her memoir, suggests what others have only whispered, that someone owed her money, did not want to pay it, and set the fire. Since everyone I interviewed described her as the most generous of souls, I hope this is not the case. At any rate, Bessie is the hotel's "playful ghost" and most agree, still in charge!

The hotel has changed hands six times since I have known it, but the owners' stories, which are attributed to Bessie, remain the same. Her favorite trick is to catch the owner or manager alone in the building, wait until they step out, and then lock them out of the hotel. Whether they go from the hotel to the annex next door through a door in the lounge or briefly step outside, Bessie will lock that door, the front door, and even the kitchen screen door which can only be locked from the inside. She also likes to play with the lights, rearrange the furniture in the rooms, make loud noises, move the netting which once hung over the beds, leave toilet seats up, drop pictures off the wall, unplug lamps (especially where the plug is located behind the bed and not easily reached), and walk in and out of guests' rooms . She is seen the most when owners are making changes and most agree she "still has a proprietary interest." Her favorite spot is in the swing on the second floor, gazing down Second Street, a spot she enjoyed for 26 years.

Now, the "water stories," most of which I heard about from former owner Dawn, but which have been corroborated over and over. Once rooms were ready for guests, Dawn would do a quick inspection. Usually, all was well, but one day there was a puddle of water under the bed. Her housekeeper assured her that it was not there when she left the room, that she had not spilled any water, but that she would clean it up.

This continued in several variations and the plumbing in the room was even checked. One time they found water dripping from the frame under the bed onto the floor, but the bedding somehow remained dry. This continued over the years, and the only solution was to keep cleaning it up. On another occasion, Molly told me about a mother who brought her middle school-age daughter to the hotel to do a report on the ghosts of the hotel. The mother seemed amused but did not really believe any of the stories she had heard. When Molly showed them the room where the water reappears, which is Room 23, she looked down and saw a puddle of water around the mother's feet. When she gently called her attention to it, the woman screamed, nearly fainted, grabbed her daughter and ran from the hotel. Molly again cleaned up the puddle. Some attribute these happenings to the woman in black with the water pitcher, some to the little black boy who often appears dripping from the cistern.

While the ghosts at the hotel are "playful and harmless," there is a "presence near the kitchen pantry" which seems malevolent. Over the years I have noticed a pattern in the accidents which occur at the hotel to the staff, most which have occurred in or near the pantry. Most of the hotel workers agree, it is a place they do not like to dwell.

I love the hotel! In fact my husband and I were married there in 1988 on the veranda at sunset by owner Marcia Rogers. I have stayed there and enjoyed many dinners, many nights in the Neptune Lounge, some sad memorial services, and even the wedding of friends and owners, Tony and Dawn Cousins, in the late 1990s. There are so many stories and odd things that have happened over the years, but I close with two that happened to my husband and me.

The first was fairly tame. One evening we found ourselves to be the last patrons in the hotel bar, and Molly asked if we would walk out the back way with her after she closed up. The hotel was empty. We said sure and after about fifteen minutes she said she was ready and walked to the front door and locked it. On her way back to us, the lights went on and off. She mumbled, "Oh no, not this again." We started to head to the back of the kitchen to leave when the front door blew open. She went back and locked it and shook it to make sure it was tight. On her way back to us the lights went on and off and on again. We quickly made our way out with Molly, and I do mean quickly!

As I said, I love the hotel. I think it is the heart and soul of Cedar Key, so my husband and I were saddened when it closed down in 2001. A couple from Texas, who owned it briefly, left suddenly one night, owing money to many. At that time we lived downtown, worked until dark, and loved to take an evening walk. One foggy night, we walked down Second Street, everything closed and quiet. When we got to the hotel we noticed lit multicolored Christmas lights on the balcony and a few lights inside. The front door was locked but we were elated that the hotel appeared to be reopening. Once home we ran into our neighbor, a realtor, and mentioned what we had seen and asked him if he knew anything about the hotel's reopening. He looked at us and laughed and accused us of "being in the wine." We assured him that we usually had a glass after our walk, but that we had had none that day. He looked at us and we again queried him on what he knew. He said, "Danny and Debbie, there are so many bills due on that building that it is locked up tight and even all the utilities have been shut off. It has to go to court." We silently walked away. We knew what we had seen and went home deep in thought. The building continued to be locked and dark for months, finally going back to the previous owners who had held the mortgage. My husband does not believe in ghosts, but admits, "It's hard to explain that one." I like to think it was a signal to us from Bessie that all will be well again, or perhaps...she was just having another one of her famous private parties!

Debra Lyon-Dye

TOUR STOP ⑬
Chapter 19

Arthur "Cush" Holston

Historic Spirit Tour Stop No. Thirteen: Read while walking back the way you came on Second Street, but stop at the Hale Building on D Street.

One of the most beloved legends of Cedar Key is that of Cush, the "Gator Man" of Cedar Key. This account is taken from Cedar Key Legends by Sally Tileston and Dottie Comfort, the vertical files of the Cedar Key Historical Society Museum, and the oral histories of many town folk. Listening to stories about Cush was such fun; weathered faces became young again as childhood memories of Cush were shared and retold.

Cush was a 'gator hunter' who strode into town from time to time, much to the delight of the children. He pranced and sang while playing the violin and soon had a parade of kids and their pets parading behind him. He set up a small camp, a house just big enough for himself, which was "air-conditioned" by having four walls which he could raise and lower to the prevailing wind. For Cush, in addition to being a hunter and musician, was also a mechanic. Cedar Key children from back then have never forgotten the time he sputtered into town in a mechanized wagon which he built from "rubber-tired wheels taken from bicycles and the engine from an old Model T."

According to "Cedar Key Legends,' he cooked at his camp for the children using secret recipes and "children from all over the island congregated for his feasts. The hungry ones were especially attended to." "Whenever Cush had money, he bought all the youngsters in town candy and ice cream cones. Then he pranced down the street, playing his fiddle and singing as the children and their dogs followed. The faster the pace, the faster he played."

Cush had no income that anyone knew of, other than fishing and hunting. Often he played in local bars, including the Island Hotel, for beer, drinks, and sandwiches. "When he played... listeners, all friendly, all loving him, gave him applause and drinks. Tapping a foot, sawing away, singing 'way off key,' he entertained. His songs were mostly old chanteys but some he made up himself. A favorite was haunting and a bit sad as he gave it."

I had a little gal on the
T-J line this mornin'

I had a little gal on the
T-J line this morning;
I had a little gal on the
T-J line...

I had no money but
I had a real good time

This mornin'---this
evenin'---so soon---

So I took her down
to the peanut stand this mornin'

So I took her down
to the peanut stand this mornin'

I took her down to the
 peanut stand

She got stuck on the
peanut man

This mornin'---this
evenin'---so soon!

Debra Lyon-Dye

According to the hanging vertical files at the Cedar Key Historical Society Museum, Cush was Milton McCain's uncle, "who staked out a small cabin near the water and became part of the community." By most accounts he was family in "some ways" to most of town, but it is said he came from the swamp and returned to the swamp after the 1950 hurricane.

The sixteen hour 1950 hurricane was "hell" for all that experienced it. A panel of local senior citizens interviewed during a 2015 'Coffee' held by the Historical Society revealed that "blessedly it did not blow the tides in, but the northeast quadrant hit the islands twice, and the winds reportedly broke the anemometer at 160 mph. Roofs were peeled off, sheets of tin sailed through the air, and many scrambled to the 'school house' during the eye to survive."

Cush was offered shelter by many in town, but chose to ride out the storm by burying himself on Hodgson Hill. Cush feared a great tidal wave. "No, this island is going to be swamped by a tidal wave. I'm going to dig in on the highest spot. That's on Hodgson's Hill." So he did, digging a hole under a palmetto clump.

Some say he was never seen again. Some say he was seen briefly, making his way back to the mainland, ill and broken. He let it be known the "misery in his bones was powerful bad." Tileston and Comfort end their account of the legend with this: "In fact, he was walking out. All he said was, 'Goodbye y'all. I'm going back where I belong. In the swamp, I'll find a gator hole and there I'll crawl in and meet my swamp brothers. I've always liked gators. Maybe I'll be good chow for them." The End.

Or was it?

After much research and searching, I found out what really happened to Cush. Suffice it to say that the legend continued and went on to inspire many other bands including the Bucksnort Barn Dance Band.

Cush, according to Florida State Archive and Libraries' Florida Folk life Collections, July-September 2008, is recalled as a, "legendary fiddler, a colorful character from Otter Creek, Florida about whom little is known. His 1960 festival performance of "We're Gonna Have a Good Time Tonight" represents one of the very few recordings known to exist." I then found links (which I have provided below) of Cush performing at folk festivals across Florida. In Florida Memories there is a recording of Cush at the Florida Folk Festival in White Springs playing the fiddle and singing several songs, including "She Gone and Left Me, Pretty Darlin,' and as if especially for Cedar Key, "I Had a Little Gal on the T-J Line This Morning." So take a listen and tap your foot with the "Gator Man" of Cedar Key.

www.floridamemory.com/items/show/241408

http://207.156.19.134/newsletter/article.aspx?articleID=1156&newsID=1025

http://fotmc.org/index.php/component/content/article/36-guest-of-honor/guest-of-honor/68-bucksnort

http://hearty42.rssing.com/chan-20556059/all_p5.html

Debra Lyon-Dye

TOUR STOP 14
Chapter 20

The Ghosts of the Hale Building

Historic Spirit Tour Stop No. Fourteen: The Hale building, Second and D Streets.

The next to the last stop on our "magical mystery tour" is the Hale Building at the corner of Second and D, also known as Highway 24. If you are still gazing at the Island Hotel, where I left you, head west towards the main intersection in town, towards what would have been "Mud Road," once the only somewhat dry corridor into town from the mainland. As of this writing this noble building, built in 1880, houses Tony's Seafood Restaurant. Originally built by Francis E. Hale, the building has had numerous owners and has housed a clothing store, real estate office, bar, grocery store, doctor's office, movie house, and several seafood restaurants. While it has had many occupants, the antics of the buildings' ghosts have over the years remained the same.

Francis E. Hale, the partner in Parsons & Hale, was born in 1845. He was elected mayor March of 1875 and served on the Cedar Keys Town Council when the council was composed of two whites and three blacks. According to Fishburne's account he, "would serve competently as mayor or alderman almost continually until after the turn of the century." That being said, to read an account of the political sparring that occurred during that time of Reconstruction, I refer you to Fishburne's "The Cedar Keys in the Civil War and Reconstruction, 1861 to 1876," available at the Museum. Mayor Hale was married to Orvilla Augusta Barnes and some of their descendants still live in Cedar Key. They are buried at the City Cemetery. She died in 1904 and Francis in 1910 at the age of 65.

The almost 4,000 square foot Hale Building features a commercial kitchen and two dining rooms downstairs, two apartments upstairs, 17 inch thick tabby walls, heart of cedar timber framing, fifteen foot ceilings, two staircases including a Savannah-style stairway which opens to the front apartment, and a lovely bricked courtyard in the back. The second floor porch was added at the turn of the century. This noble structure has witnessed the comings, goings and changes of Cedar Key for over a century. While surviving fires, hurricanes and other threats, it has never suffered the neglect of its historical sisters.

One of the building's many occupants witnessed the last quarter of the last century in Cedar Key and observed that Cedar Key in the 1970s was still a "sleepy fishing village." School teacher, mother, doctor's wife, restaurant owner, and librarian Janice Coupe wrote in her book, *Paradise Lost, A Cedar Key Memoir,* "Nothing about the sleepy fishing village spoke of progress, and the inhabitants were happy with things just as they were, I too loved Cedar Key just as it was..." Janice's book is an account of the events and therefore changes that occurred on the islands from 1972 to 2004. Janice was a friend of mine and while some say her account is bitter, I find it painfully accurate: hurricanes and even worse "no name" storms, telephone tapping and lawsuits, commercial fishing restrictions and a statewide net ban, the coming of condominiums and development of the island into a day, week, month destination, and the inevitable life changes of growing older. Janice, like Eliza Hearn, did not write with her "rose colored glasses on." Her other book, however, *Gourmet Cooking, Sixty Miles From a Lemon,* is a fabulous cookbook and delightful account of her days owning and running the 150 seat Heron Restaurant from New Year's Eve 1981 to 2004. Think local antique pieces, twinkling faux kerosene lamps, walls lined with historical black and white photos, pink and white tablecloths, waitresses in long calico skirts with white Victorian tops and aprons, luscious local seafood, and bud vases of pink carnations. Service, often by one of Janice's daughters, was professional, welcoming and efficient. God, I still miss that elegant restaurant and its fine cuisine.

Tearing my thoughts from Martha and Jimmy Allen's hand-picked crab meat, I will now give an account, or rather Janice's account of the spirits or ghosts of the Heron Building. Janice and her husband purchased the Hale Building in 1981 from Dr. Edwin Andrews. The physicians had shared a medical practice in the back half of the building, a door opening onto D Street. Dr. Andrews retired and Dr. George Coupe took over the practice. For a while they shared the building with a group called the Cedar Keyhole, a "group of arts and crafters who had formed a cooperative in 1978." When Janice wanted to open a restaurant in the front of the building, the Keyhole had to move out and shared space in Colson's Auto Parts. (Artist Catherine Christie eventually purchased Colson's, added a second floor, and then donated the building to the cooperative, where it remains today.)

Like most residents of Cedar Key, Janice and her cook and wait staff were familiar with Cedar Key's ghost stories: the headless horseman, Annie Simpson and many others. For years they shrugged off the toilet mysteriously flushing upstairs and the opening and closing of doors when no one was there with a, "It's just a ghost." But finally, when things started happening directly to them, they reluctantly began to believe.

One morning, Janice and fellow worker Fritz were readying for lunch when several kitchen utensils flew out of a crock on a shelf near where Janice was standing, and sailed across the room some ten feet towards Fritz. They fell to the floor before hitting her and Fritz in surprise asked, "…did you throw those at me?" Janice replied, "Don't be silly, would I throw things at you?" While surprised and puzzled, they both had to return to work. The next day, Janice was at the cookin' stove, when several of her cooking spoons rose up out of a jar over to where Fritz was standing. Both began to get nervous. Fritz revealed that she did not believe in Cedar Key ghost stories but that when she and another worker went to relax in the back Rose Room, "something brushed the back of my leg." Janice assured her that there had to be "some good explanation." Janice wrote, "Weird things became commonplace," including the feeling "that something very cold was directly behind me watching over my shoulder while I worked."

Late one night after midnight, Janice's daughter Patty came downstairs visibly upset. "Mom, I was just stopped in the hall upstairs." Confused her mother asked if someone was upstairs. "No, not someone, something. I was hurrying to get back down here because it's so scary up there late at night. I was rushing down the hall, and suddenly I was stopped in my tracks like I had run into a wall. It lasted only a moment, and then I continued. There wasn't anything there at all. Some invisible force wouldn't let me go forward. It was something invisible that wouldn't let me move." Unexplained things continued and the years went by.

Debra Lyon-Dye

Now to one of my favorite stories. As you know, if you have ever worked in a restaurant, you do setups the night before so all is ready in the morning. The Heron was no exception, this setup including the placing of fresh pink carnations in tiny bud vases on each table. But apparently the resident ghost had other ideas as the staff would arrive to find the bud vases snipped of each and every flower, only the stem remaining. Sometimes the flowers were on the floor, but more often than not there was no trace of them. Continuing to take "weird things in stride," Janice told her staff to put the flowers in the cooler at night. They were never snipped again. Recently I asked a former waitress from the restaurant named Mary, why the ghost didn't go in the cooler and she simply replied, "I don't know, I'm not a ghost!"

According to Janice more supernatural activities occurred over the years: vanishing patrons, rearranged place settings, someone walking by the pass-through window, workers who refused to come back, especially one particular air-conditioner repairman named Kenny.

After Janice sold her restaurant several different restaurants used the space. In 1997 my daughter waitressed in the building for Peter Stefani. They used a collection of taped music to provide ambiance. Many nights my daughter came home complaining of a busy night coupled with the music's having a life of its own, startling guests with loud or strange music, only to find the originally selected tape still inside.

For a very brief period of time a friend named Bob decided to do renovations on the restaurant and have a bakery. While working under the sink, he called to his partner to hand him a wrench, which she did. He finished work and looked for his partner. She had returned to their home much earlier and had never handed him the wrench. At least the ghost could be helpful.

Cedar Key Spirit Tour

From 2004 to 2016 Judy Duvall owned the grand building, living upstairs as well as operating an insurance business from the second floor. She leased the downstairs to a restaurant. When I interviewed her in the upstairs apartment she repeated the same occurrences that several other townspeople have shared: a child's crying on the back stairs, things disappearing one night and reappearing the next, noises when there is no one else in the building, the cold chill of someone standing behind her. But she added quite a few of her own. The curtain over the window above the back stairs that fell so many times she gave up and left it down. Mirrors that come crashing down into pieces. A roll of toilet paper winding from the bathroom, down the hall, around a corner, into the living room. But she too says she has never felt afraid. She does, however, hang tight to the railing as she once felt a presence on the stairs, not holding her back but giving her a slight nudge.

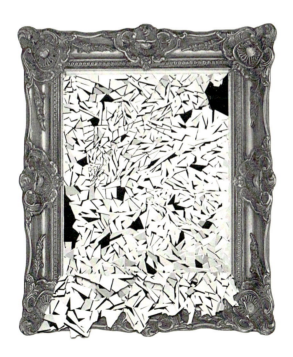

Perhaps her strangest encounter occurred in 2012 while watching a surveillance video with the owner of the restaurant downstairs. "Eric was trying to see who had played a trick on him some time in the night, putting a pile of long-handled lighters on the floor by the kitchen door. We watched it together. The camera is set off by motion. The kitchen was pitch black and there are no windows, but as we watched a white ball of light came in through the wall bouncing wildly like a rubber ball. It finally went out the back of the kitchen wall into the back dining room and then outdoors to the courtyard. It then disappeared. Just remembering that raises the hair on my arms. I've also seen lights bouncing late at night, which I guess are orbs, while sitting on the porch out over the street. I like to sit out there alone at night when it is quiet." She repeats, "But I've never felt afraid."

Several minutes after Judy related these stories to me in her upstairs apartment, a large handsome six foot antique cabinet in the corner of the room near where we were sitting emitted a very, very loud crack. Judy and I looked at one other.

Interview over, time to go!

Chapter 21

TOUR STOP 15

Cedar Key Historical Society Museum

Historic Spirit Tour Stop No. Fifteen: Cedar Key Historical Society Museum, Second and D Streets.

The Lutterloh Building has been home to the museum since it opened in 1979. Once a private residence, the building has been used as an army depot, service station, restaurant, club, city library, and gift shop. The building was donated to the Historical Society in 1978 by Gertrude Teas for the preservation of the "heritage of her beloved village." In 1995, the Andrews House, former home of the Standard Manufacturing Company's Fiber Factory, was moved from the east end of Second Street to its present site. In 2007 The Lutterloh Building was painstakingly restored. (When we first came to Cedar Key we rented the apartment above the museum. Before renovations, the floor slope was so pronounced you would get out of bed in the morning and from the back bedroom actually walk downhill to the front door.)

The museum has only one part-time person on staff, but operates with a cadre of volunteers. Docents are trained in the tradition of Ruth Wagner, the original docent who served for fourteen years. They are helpful, pleasant, and knowledgeable.

I finish this book at the site of the museum, because it is there that further questions can be answered, most of the books I have cited can be purchased, and exhibits can further enhance your experience. It is also fitting that I end at the museum with a ghost story, that of "The Chain Smoking Ghost."

When I began working on this book and doing my Spirit Tours, two board members tentatively approached me. They wondered if I had had any strange experiences in the museum and I said, "No." After a little coaxing, and in whispers they told me that on several occasions they and other board members had smelled smoke in the Andrews Building. Of course, as in all old wooden buildings, the smell of smoke was very alarming. A thorough search was done, but nothing was found emitting smoke and the fire alarms had not gone off. This happened on and off several times to several people. Then they added that while upstairs in the Andrews Building Board Room there were noises in the other rooms. That sometimes chairs fell over and there were other bumping noises.

Then, museum visitors began to make comments, several of which I have personally heard while serving as docent: "Is the back building haunted? When I was in the back building I was not alone. Someone has been smoking in the back building. I smell the clothes of someone who smokes a lot, but no one is there. Do you have someone here who chain smokes?"

Well, in fact, there used to be two women who frequented the museum, both of whom chain smoked, and both passed away. Could it be...? The occurrences continue.

So, I leave you in front of the museum, which I hope you will visit for more Cedar Key history. I hope you have enjoyed your tour, which I always managed to finish just at dark. But before I leave you alone here on the street, I wish to end with a Haiku, like I did all of my Spirit Tours. This is a Haiku by Miss Verona Watson, artist, writer, and Cedar Key native, taken from her *Haiku and Mini-Thoughts* published in 1982.

If you see a lass

Walking in the mist

Walk with her

But do not touch her.

With that, I leave you. Good night!

Debra Lyon-Dye

Acknowledgements

My inspiration for my historic spirit tours was Haint Mistress Donnamarie Emmert, a retired teacher and historian in Abingdon, Virginia. One evening, thoroughly enjoying her ghost tour, I noticed that the majority of participants were young people. Enticed by the tales of ghosts and spirits, they were captured by the fascinating history of the 1700s town. In turn, I learned more about Abingdon in that tour than I had in all the twelve years I had spent there. The proverbial light bulb blinked on above my head--this is what I could do to interest the youth of Cedar Key (and others, of course) in the rich history of our island home. Haint Mistress Donnamarie, ever the teacher, sat me down one afternoon and for several hours schooled me in the art of leading historical spirit tours. I am forever indebted.

But an idea only goes so far without a cheerleader and I had two, my husband, Danny, and Cedar Key native, Brenda Baylor Coulter.

My husband supports me in all things, is my first editor, and as our granddaughters will assure you, is a prince. He is also my in-house "IT" guy and the calm to my fury. Merci.

Brenda Coulter taught many years at Cedar Key School, including the four years I taught there, but our primary connection was at Christ Episcopal Church. Once I told her about my idea, a historical spirit tour and subsequent book, a Sunday never went by that she didn't say, "Miss Debbie, how's that book coming?" I mean, never a Sunday went by; she had a confidence in me that I didn't have in myself. She trusted me with her island home's story. I had to do it! She pointed me in the right direction, opened doors to local senior citizens that I might not have found, answered a thousand questions, set up an interview with her husband, Henry, and read my rough draft. This book simply would not be without her. So to Brenda, the little girl whose back yard was the islands around Cedar Key, the little girl who carried bobby pins for shear pins for her boat motor, the fellow teacher who made me a copy of Dottie Comfort and Sally Tilestons' little book of legends, my friend, a multitude of thank you's!

Debra Lyon-Dye

I will now attempt to thank those who contributed to four years of research on Cedar Key history, local ghost stories, favorite legendary people of the area, and fact checking: Molly Brown, Bill Roberts, Dr. Kenneth Sasserman, Lindon Lindsey, Toni Collins, Doreen Bauer, Oliver Bauer, Beth Davis, Thelma McCain, Judy Duvall, Dr. John Andrews, Ken Young, Molly Jubitz, Bill Bale, Molly Cowart, Galina Brinkley, Laura Jean Delaino, Henry Coulter, Jo Ann Baylor Phillips, Stanley Bair, Pam Wadley, Lois Benninghoff, Jack Watson, Bizz Paeth, Helen Parramore, and Pat Deverin. I am so grateful!

When I was ready to take my historic spirit tour "on the road," four local business people stand out as my biggest supporters: Judy Duvall, who offered to let me do tours from the courtyard of the Hale Building, which she owned; Nancy Stephens, owner of Déjà vu; and Doreen and Oliver Bauer, owners of the Faraway Inn, who promoted my tours tirelessly. Thank you for everything!

Suffice it to say that when I actually began my tours downtown, "red tape" led me to the Cedar Key Historical Society Museum Board. While I had been a member of the Society, I was urged by some to present to the board the idea of my tour. The board agreed unanimously to allow me to lead my tours from the museum, once they approved the content for accuracy, in the spirit of bringing in a wider audience. This was truly a blessing and I thank then director Molly Cowart and board members: Linda Dale, John McPherson, George Sresovich, Marianne McEuen, Ken Young, Doris Hellermann, Ada Lang, George Oakley, Brenda Coulter, Jackie Padgett, Minnie Crevasse, and Julie Stevens. I would like to also thank current Director Galina Brinkley, who has been so helpful, and board members Dr. John Andrews, Bill Bale, Doreen Bauer, and Pam Wadley. The museum's support has been humbling.

Finally, putting my tour and collection of historical accounts on paper was a vast undertaking. My goal was historical accuracy and I would like to again thank the following readers who took their time to read all or part of my manuscript: Danny Dye, my Aunt Pat Lyon Jones, Brenda Coulter, Henry Coulter, Jo Ann Baylor

Phillips, Laura Jean Delaino, Doreen Bauer, Stanley Bair, Judy Duvall, Bill Bale, Dr. John Andrews, Karen Sroka, mentors Bunny Medeiros and Kathy Shearer, and editor, Sally Turner Baylor. Finally, hats off to my Graphic Designer, Stephen Wolfsberger, who made my book shine!

Though the words are often used, this Cedar Key history has been truly a labor of love.

Partial Bibliography

Andrews, John. W., M.D. *Cedar Key Fiber and Brush Factory, "From the Tree to Thee."* Ocala, FL: Atlantic Publishing Group, Inc., 2016.

Collins, Toni C. *Cedar Keys Light Station*. Chiefland, FL: Suwannee River Publishing Co., 2011.

Coupe, Janice. *Paradise Lost, A Cedar Key Memoir*. Eureka, CA: Garden Court Press, 2009.

Day, P. H. *Destination Cedar Key*. Cedar Key, FL: As told to and written by Jennie Stevens, 2002.

Fishburne, Charles C., Jr. *The Cedar Keys in the Civil War and Reconstruction: 1861-1876*. Cedar Key, FL: Sea Hawk Publications, 1982.

Fishburne, Charles C., Jr. *Cedar Key Booming: 1877-1886*. Cedar Key, FL: Sea Hawk Publications, 1982.

Fishburne, Charles, C., Jr. *Cedar Key: Prelude to the Twentieth Century, 1891 to 1900*. Cedar Key, FL: Sea Hawk Publications, 1982.

Fishburne, Charles C., Jr. *The Cedar Keys in the 19th Century*. Cedar Key, FL: Cedar Key Historical Society Publication, 2004.

Hearn, Eliza. *Diary*. (Died 1910). Cedar Key Historical Society Archives.

Lindsey, Lindon J. *Cemeteries of Levy and Other Counties*. Cedar Key, FL: Self -published, 1994.

Moore, Joyce Elson. *Haunt Hunters Guide to Florida*. Sarasota, FL: Pineapple Press, 1998.

Muir, John. *A Thousand Mile Walk to the Gulf*. New York, New York: Houghton Mifflin Co., original 1916, paperback 1998.

Oickle, Alvin F. *The Cedar Keys Hurricane of 1896: Disaster at Dawn*. Charleston, SC: The History Press, 2009.

Tileston, Sally and Dottie Comfort. *Cedar Key Legends, Volume I*. Cedar Key, FL: Self-published, 1960s.